blueprints for the soul

why we need emotion in architecture

Nick Moss and Barbara Iddon

RIBA ⫶ **Publishing**

© Nick Moss and Barbara Iddon, 2024

Published by RIBA Publishing, 66 Portland Place, London, W1B 1AD

ISBN 9781915722386

The rights of Nick Moss and Barbara Iddon to be identified as the Authors of this Work have been asserted in accordance with the Copyright, Designs and Patents Act 1988 sections 77 and 78.

British Library Cataloguing-in-Publication Data

A catalogue record for this book is available from the British Library.

Commissioning Editor: Elizabeth Webster
Publishing Co-ordinator: Flo Armitage-Hookes
Production: Jane Rogers
Designed by Mercer Design, London
Printed and bound by Short Run Press, Exeter

While every effort has been made to check the accuracy and quality of the information given in this publication, neither the Author nor the Publisher accept any responsibility for the subsequent use of this information, for any errors or omissions that it may contain, or for any misunderstandings arising from it.

www.ribapublishing.com

contents

about the authors

Nick Moss is the owner of Nick Moss Architects, a multi-award-winning practice based in Manchester.

Nick studied at Liverpool University and became a chartered architect in 2003. He began his architectural career working for prominent design studios Stephenson Bell and subsequently Hodder and Partners, until setting up his own studio in 2012.

With experience that ranges from restoring hidden gems to reshaping key parts of our towns and cities, Nick's practice has a strong emphasis on enhancing community, culture and place to create designs that interact beautifully with their environment.

Nick has served as president of Manchester Society of Architects and on the RIBA North West Regional Council. He's a visiting lecturer and critic at a number of universities.

Barbara Iddon studied at Manchester Metropolitan University, gaining a degree in social science. Subsequently, Barbara worked in community development, tenant participation and place identity strategy, where her lively, pragmatic and innovative approach resulted in many successful bids and outcomes.

She's currently a writer, counsellor and company director.

Barbara's many years of study, observation and experience relating to a wide range of social strata, abilities, cultures and needs, combined with regular interaction with the Manchester architect community, creates a rare and often refreshing perspective on the human condition in relation to the built environment.

introduction

There's a relationship you've had since the day you were born and you'll have it until the day you die. But there's a problem in this relationship: you might say it's become dysfunctional. The relationship is between you and the state of the buildings that surround you.

You may not walk around our towns and cities lamenting this fact. You may not register it at all. But in the corner of your being, you detect an undercurrent that something isn't quite right, and it bothers you. A sort of vague dissatisfaction. A strange compulsion to avert your eyes. A feeling of being unpleasantly overwhelmed or oppressed without knowing why.

The built environment is invading you with its impoverishment of emotional, aesthetic and spiritual impact. Good architecture can impress itself upon our hearts and inspire satisfaction. It invites us to experience a sense of beauty, engagement and memory; something greater than ourselves.

Imagine for a moment you're walking down a tree-lined country lane. It's spring and the first bright day for many weeks. Sunlight dapples the scene as you take in the scent of pine and grass and earth. You contemplate the spring flowers carpeting the ground. Birdsong fills the air. There's a sense of life bursting forth everywhere you look. Despite the fact you can still see your breath, a feeling of joy and connectedness washes through you. You feel calm and whole.

We don't question why nature matters. We implicitly understand that nature feeds us metaphorically as well as literally. Nowhere was this more evident than in the lockdowns endured during the earlier stages of the Covid-19 pandemic, when city dwellers became ever more desperate to leave the urban sprawl and get into the green. Human beings are highly attuned to the sensory inputs of the natural environment. On the large scale, we respond to the sight of a captivating view. On the small scale, our senses can come alive at the sight of richly painted flowers, the pungent green smell of freshly cut grass or the song of a blackbird. For all but the most diehard of urban dwellers, nature provides us with intense feelings of sensual and emotional (and some would say spiritual) fulfilment. Nature can induce feelings of aesthetic appreciation, awe and wonder. The visual patterns of the natural environment deliver a sense of emotional ease. It could be argued that our response to nature – those hard-wired capacities, which have developed over millennia – forms the roots of our response to everything in the environment.

The above isn't stated so we can engage in a back-to-nature fantasy. It's to make the point that we're hard-wired to respond to certain stimuli, whether that be a first glimpse of the Grand Canyon, viewing a stunning work of art, or standing in a cathedral. Our response to beauty, to the right things in the right place, is part of what makes life worth living.

Most of us don't live in the countryside. Most of us live and/or work around lots of buildings. Over the last century, many of those buildings have become increasingly functional, featureless and downright unappealing. They're simply anti-human. The power of architecture to inspire, move and delight has been under attack for a long time and for a lot of different reasons. But that doesn't mean it's stopped mattering. Emotion in architecture matters because it satisfies and encompasses the human condition and offers a glimpse into the transcendent. Emotion in architecture allows us to admire, appreciate and engage.

If positive emotion in architecture produces the above, it isn't difficult to work out what its opposite does. When the beauty we perceive in the natural environment is absent in the built one, it forms part of a negative downward spiral that can have a devastating effect. When our natural capacities for aesthetic appreciation are quashed, instead of feeling inspired, we feel imprisoned. Instead of feeling uplifted, we feel depressed. Instead of feeling liberated, we feel oppressed. Instead of feeling connected, we feel isolated. Bad buildings, like undiagnosed high blood pressure or type two diabetes, silently rob us of energy, health and wellbeing.

This isn't about the Lloyd's building versus Villa Savoye, or the Louvre Pyramid versus the Isokon building. Indeed, if you're not connected to the world of architecture, you may not even know what or where some of those buildings are. This isn't about the lofty projects academics and critics are so keen to discuss. It's about the buildings we experience every day as we go about our business, the ones we live and work in. The houses and shops, the offices and cafés, the schools and centres. It's about the fact so many of them are letting us down.

Emotion is different from reasoning or knowledge. It's a sensory state akin to the five senses, but while other senses register the state of the external world, emotion registers the state of the internal world. It's what causes us to feel alive. It's what allows us to appreciate such things as beauty, wonder and awe.

There are a number of ways in which a building can generate emotion. Emotion through association generally relates to a sense of history, whether that be societal or personal. We humans love places

3

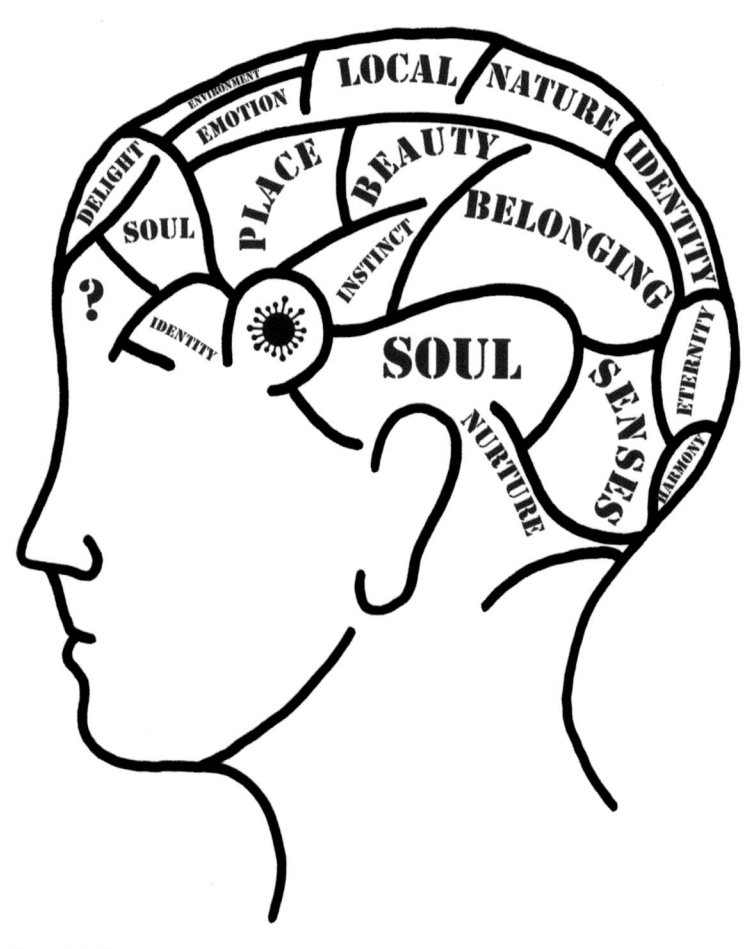

Figure 0.1 The Phrenology of Architecture. There are many factors to be considered in the creation of a better built environment.

of historical interest and, as we step into them, we feel the past as well as see it, which both grounds and fulfils us. It resonates. Even just passing by a building with history makes many people feel securely rooted in a past they intuitively know forms an integral part of their identity. Emotional association, whether positive or negative, can also be present in buildings that have a personal connection, such as our old school or the house we grew up in.

Instinctive emotion relates to concepts such as hearth, home, security and belonging. Even though it's not necessary in a home with efficient central heating, a hearth with some kind of fire in it is still important to large numbers of people.

Aesthetic emotion is a direct emotional response to a building in the here and now. It encompasses such feelings as delight, joy, calm, inspiration, affection and belonging. While the previous categories are easily quantifiable, this last category is the most nebulous, which may well explain the scarcity of any form of literature about it. Emotion can't be adequately described by intellect; perhaps this is the reason we rely on writers, musicians, artists and dwindling numbers of architects to do the job for us. With aesthetic emotion difficult to quantify or even describe, people have become jumpy and reluctant about nailing their emotional colours to the mast. Indeed, it's often in more general works concerning broader societal issues, such as David Goodhart's *Head, Hand, Heart* – a book about dignity and status in the 21st century – that one is likely to find a paragraph or passing comment that dares to offer a perspective on the subject.[1]

Aesthetic emotion in architecture isn't easily defined or explained, but just because something isn't easy to define or explain, nor even registered consciously, doesn't mean it isn't important. Emotion is the fourth dimension of architecture and yet all too often within the profession, beauty has become the love that dare not speak its name. Architecture is unique in the field of human endeavour – the one activity where science and art can join together like lovers in a passionate embrace.

If we have the means to do so, most of us refuse to tolerate the disagreeable, featureless and utilitarian in our everyday lives, the parts of our lives we feel we have some control over. Every year, the British people spend billions of pounds on such things as cosmetics, beauty treatments, furnishings, art and jewellery. While a proportion of this money may be spent for functional reasons, the greater part of it is to enhance the beauty and comfort of the individual and their personal surroundings. Millions of people visit museums, galleries and buildings of interest. If proof were needed that the drive to be embraced by beauty and emotional appeal exists, it abounds in the activities of the population.

Beauty can arouse a state of happiness, satisfaction and compelling positive engagement in the beholder. Most succinctly, it might be described as generating a feeling of pleasure. At its most transcendent, it can move us to tears.

But it's the invocation of those feelings that concerns us here. The means by which our innate sense of beauty can gain the fulfilment it craves. Beauty is famously difficult to define and there are many facets to its encouragement. As architect Louis Kahn said, 'Design is not making beauty, beauty emerges from selection, affinities, integration, love.'[2] Beauty is the unfolding of an internal order which results from and resonates with hard-wired human sensibilities; it's not as subjective as we are often led to believe. Beauty in architecture happens when what our senses register 'out there' perfectly reconciles with the natural and as yet mysterious receptors we feel inside. While science engages in an ongoing quest to identify and describe the components of beauty and emotional satisfaction in architecture, history has already provided them. We'll propose that this empirical thread demonstrates there are three eternal qualities crucial to the fulfilment of aesthetic appeal and emotional satisfaction in our everyday buildings, qualities that can lead us to generate infinitely inventive, creative and beautiful architecture. Each one is fundamental to producing a whole that's greater than the sum of its parts, a whole that satisfies our hunger.

Those who deny the need for emotion and beauty in the built environment pass sentence on us all. A building, unlike a painting, doesn't hang on the wall of someone's house. It's there for all the world to see. In many ancient societies, when a member of the tribe was suffering from depression, despair or lack of meaning it was generally known as 'loss of soul', a useful phrase to describe much that surrounds us in terms of the built environment. The conditions and pressures leading to this point are complex and many, but the solutions are simpler than one might think.

Architecture is an art when one consciously or unconsciously creates aesthetic emotion in the atmosphere and when this environment produces wellbeing.[3]

LUIS BARRAGÁN, ARCHITECT.

welcome to the rabbit hole

Remember that bit in *The Matrix* where Neo, who senses something isn't quite right with the world, finally gets to meet Morpheus? Morpheus tells Neo that if he wants to know what the Matrix is, he has to see it for himself. If he takes the blue pill, this is where it ends: everything will go back to being the way it was. If he takes the red pill, he gets to discover how deep the rabbit hole goes.[1]

This is your red pill moment. Read on and it's possible you'll never see things in quite the same way again. Stop now and everything stays the same. Apart from the fact you might be a little put out about buying a book you're not going to read.

You've chosen to continue. Welcome to the rabbit hole. Don't worry, you're not about to see a green-screen world full of scrolling digits, although as it happens, some architects report that's sort of what happens to them. Come their third year of study, architecture students often really struggle to understand what the heck it's all about. Then, one day they step into the street and turn into the architectural equivalent of Neo when he sees everything in code for the first time. At that moment, it all finally makes sense to them. The psychologist Melanie Klein believed that there's no gain without loss, no loss without gain. At the very point of acquisition, they can lose something, too.

We have a natural tendency to ignore things we believe we can't do anything about. Chances are, like them or loathe them, you just accept the structures you see as a fact of life. Who can blame you? It's not as if you can have them demolished or cover them with a nice throw if you don't like them. But maybe it's time to look a little more closely. Maybe it's time to let the scales fall from your eyes. Because we really need to do something about this stuff. There are places that shout their disdain for you and places that wrap you in their warm and tender love. Unfortunately, the warm and tender love is

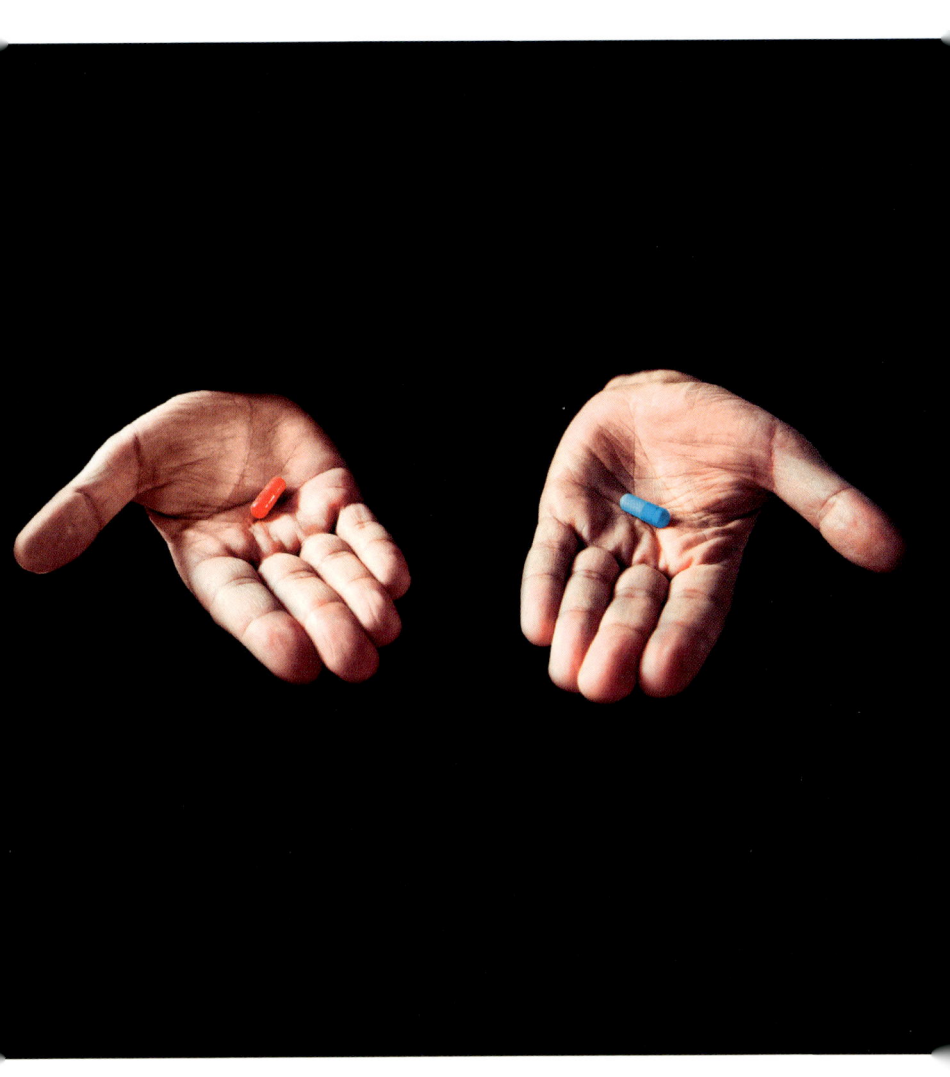

Figure 1.1 Like Neo in *The Matrix*, are you ready to take the red pill?

getting thin on the ground and it's not doing you any good. So here's a little something to get you started.

Firstly, there's a difference between a building and architecture. Basically, if it's bad, it's a building, if it's good, it's architecture. We don't need bad buildings. Bad buildings are hurting us. We do need good architecture. It's time to talk about the difference. And to do that, we have to go back in time. Way, way back.

Marcus Vitruvius Pollio, known as Vitruvius, was a 1st-century BCE Roman author, architect and civil and military engineer. He developed three principles of architecture, which have never been improved upon in over 2,000 years.

The first is *Utilitas* (Commodity), which relates to function. A building must be designed to accommodate the kinds of activities that will take place in it. Imagine you're designing a hotel. There are a host of considerations: access, parking, reception, food and beverage, housekeeping and so on. Then there's access to an outside view, ventilation, lighting and heating. Privacy and security, emergency escape. All these things come under the heading of *Utilitas*.

The second is *Firmitas* (Firmness). The structure has to be safe and able to withstand both its own weight and the weight of what will be placed within it, whether that be people, equipment or both. It has to be able to cope with whatever weather conditions are likely to occur in the country where it will be built.

But the third, *Venustas* (Delight), is what turns a building into architecture. The functions and structural elements have to be synthesised together to create a piece of architecture, the same way a composer synthesises any number of sounds to create a beautiful symphony. At its most basic, a building is a structure or shelter that serves a function. A style applied to its façade doesn't necessarily make it architecture, although it can be beneficial in terms of being pleasing to the eye, at least initially. Architecture embodies an idea that informs the whole building. It represents an ideal in the spaces, materials and structure that come together to create an experience, whatever the age or style in which it's been created.

There are plenty of books that describe all the technical details and factors that underpin good architecture, if that's something you want to explore. But even if you do, it still won't fully explain the aforementioned symphony of delight. Reducing elements to their constituent parts doesn't necessarily explain the whole. Take falling in love.

Love produces profound changes in the body; it's a kind of hormonal tidal wave. When we're besotted, our bodies flood with chemicals that make us long to be with the object of our desire every moment of the day. The very thought of it fills us with the feel-good factor. We also produce chemicals that render us impervious to the faults of our beloved. No doubt anyone who's ever been in the first flush of love will testify to that. For the neuroscientist, romantic love can appear to be nothing more than a kind of hormonal insanity that makes us dependent, delusional and irrational long enough to mate and then protect vulnerable offspring. Science and medical writer Rita Carter comments that it's a less than sensible way to organise a society.[2]

Knowledge of these constituent parts (these powerful chemicals like dopamine and oxytocin) can't make us fall in love, allow us to avoid falling in love, or make us act more rationally when we are in love. Neither can it explain the whole experience of romantic love, which is greater than the sum of these constituent parts, or the millions of incredible, enriching experiences, poems, novels, works of art and films this 'madness' has created. Without romantic love there'd be

A PARIQVADRATA SVPERFICIE HVMÃI CORPORIS PERDISTINCTÃ EO NÃTVRÃLI CENTRO
VMBILICI CIRCVLVM EXCIPERE: ET IN EO QVADRATVM MINOREM INSCRIBERE, FIGÃ

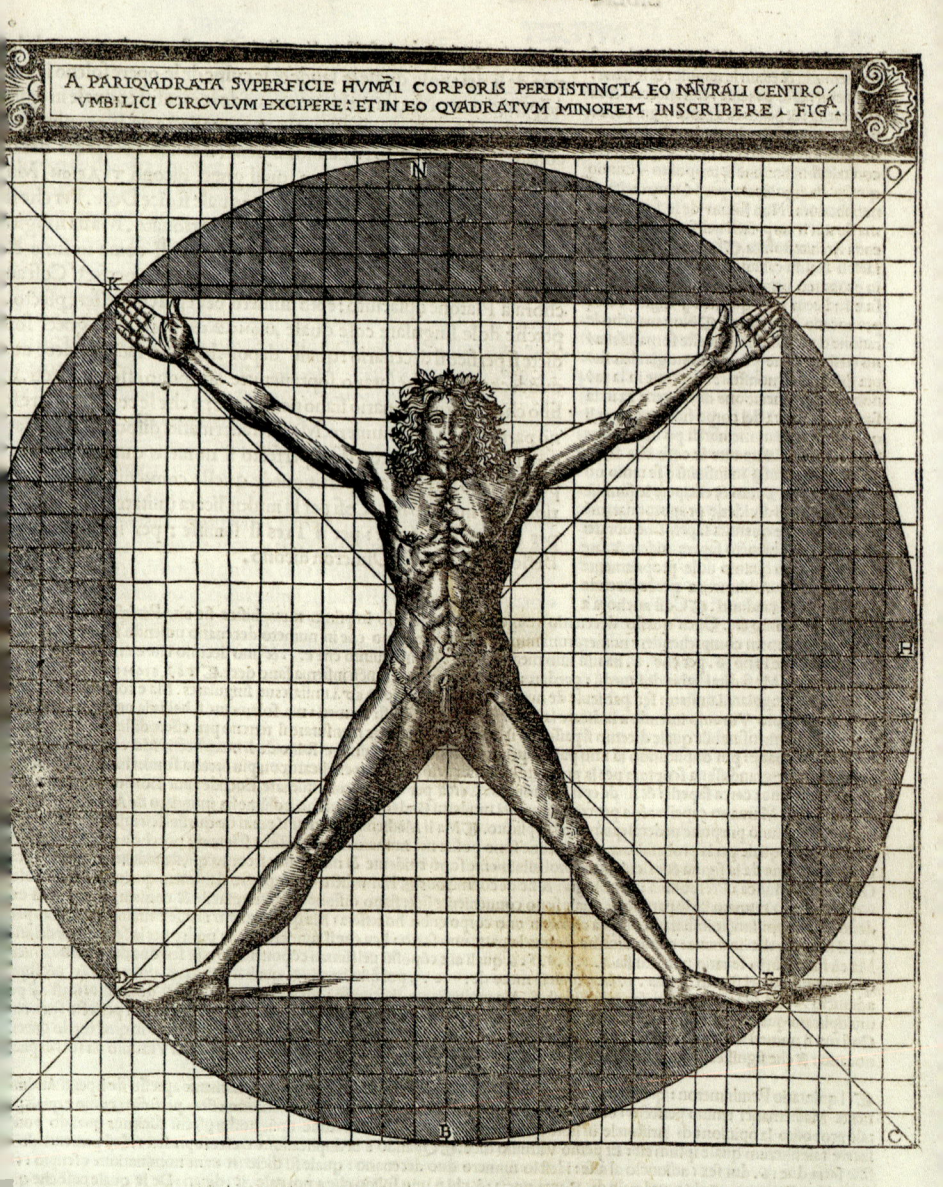

Adunchā ſi la natura ha coſi cõpoſito il corpo del homo: Queſte lectione ſi forſe altramẽte ſi uoleſſe qualcuno fuſſeno di
ūctēp ordine: como alcuni phiſici hano ſcripto: Ma per le ſupradicte: ſi etiam per le pſente ratione che Vitruuio qua inſeque:
ſi pareno aſai explicate: Ma conſiderando che potreſſemo fare grandiſſima ſcriptura in explicare la inſequentia de quiſti nu
eri: le quale coſe a me pareno facile: & coſi penſo debeno eſſere a tuti li periti de Arithmetica: cum ſia apertamẽte ſi tracta
r la compoſitione de li numeri ſimplici: potere peruenire a formare uno compoſito de qualũq; quantita uoglia ſi ſia: Poi
e epſo ut alias ſupra diximus: per potere epſa quantita diuidere proportionatamente in diuerſe portione in le quale ſi dice con
ſterela ſymmetria: Et di queſto Vitruuio da lo exemplo præcipue in li noſtri humani corpi trouarſe: nel per epſo potere perdu

cere tute le ratione de li numeri & proportio
tione de le ſymmetrie tanto per potere com
ponere quanto etiam diſcomponere una in
tegra quantita numerabile: ſi como in uno
corpo de uno animale: uel de uno homo
cõmenſurare ogni membri principali: & in
tendere le in apparente coſe & internodatio
ne & altre parte como molti phiſici hano
deſcripto: ut puta da uno brazo uno cubi
to: & dal cubito: la mane: & da epſa li di

aduncha ſi la natura ha coſi compoſito il corpo del homo ſi como cõ
proportione li menbri de epſo reſpondeno a la ſũma figuratione.
um ſia li antiquí ſi uedeno hauer conſtituito quella: acio che ancho
a in le perfectione de ciaſcuni membri de le opere le figure habiano
la uniuerſa ſpecie la exactione de la cõmenſuratione. Aduncha cũ

no Taj Mahal, no *Romeo and Juliet*, no *The Kiss*. In a similar vein, while good architecture – architecture that creates emotion – can and must embody certain qualities in the first instance, ultimately, it can't be reduced to a checklist.

Right now, if you were asked to think of a couple of buildings you like and a couple that you don't, you'd be able to call them up pretty quickly. There are all kinds of reasons you might like them: personal, associative, aesthetic or even downright quirky. Likewise the reasons you don't. If you're more experienced in the world of design, your appreciation might well have supplementary leanings. But everyone can benefit from exhuming a more primal, intuitive state of mind that focuses the knowing faculties because that will allow you to experience what's really happening in your body when you engage with the built environment.

There are many legitimate reasons for liking a place. But ask yourself, what is it about the building itself that makes me feel good about it, that makes me want to look at it or be there? If you think about what it is you like about the first two and don't like about the second two, you'll learn something about yourself and the buildings. That gives you a simple basis on which to increase your sensing faculties. But it doesn't stop there.

Figure 1.2 *Vitruvian Man*, by Cesare Cesariano, based on the work of Vitruvius, a Roman architect who believed the human body to be a model of symmetry and harmony: the centre of 'cosmic geometry'.

We all have preferences with regard to styles that often chime with our individual personalities:

Author A: When I first went into the Sagrada Família in Barcelona, I cried for about ten minutes. I just couldn't stop. It was so beautiful, joyous and I felt like I was surrounded by love.

Author B: I think Gaudí's a bit Disney.

Our age, too, can influence our likes and dislikes. Over time, we can develop an inner idea about what buildings should look like. Older people are often more likely to prefer the older styles of buildings because that's what they grew up with, whereas a younger person who's grown up around lots of contemporary architecture is more likely to be comfortable with it. And, of course, it's possible to like a style of building because you feel like you're supposed to, or because it's fashionable. The fact is, if you're willing to examine your preconceptions and put them to one side, you don't necessarily need a list of what makes good architecture because you already know.

We all have an innate sense of what works and what doesn't, of proportion and rightness and the message the architect is sending to us. It just tends to get buried under the leaf litter of life. We're hard-wired to respond to certain patterns and qualities in our buildings, but it's like a muscle we never use, so it becomes weak. We might not be able to register our faculties with the degree and precision of appreciation that an expert can summon, but we can still get the gist. Chances are, you'd rather visit a coastal Cornish village than the industrial estate down the

Figure 1.3 Sagrada Família, Barcelona, designed by Antoni Gaudí. Architecture can stir different emotions in different people.

road. And you'd prefer happening upon the Sydney Opera House rather than the Amazon warehouse just off the Milnrow exit of the M62, which suggests you already sense more than you might think you do.

There has perhaps been no greater advocate for the notion that we humans can instinctively recognise satisfying and uplifting architecture than architect, writer, teacher and theorist Christopher Alexander. In *The Nature of Order,* he describes an experiment that points to this innate sense on a basic level. The subject is shown simple paired objects such as a glass salt shaker with a metal top and a glass Heinz ketchup bottle, two spoons of slightly different design, a pair of scissors and a can of rubber cement. Rather than being asked which they like best, the subjects are asked which object most represents them as a whole being. In the examples listed here, 80 to 90% of people asked chose the same object, regardless of factors such as profession or culture. This sense of wholeness in an object, whether a salt shaker or a building, Christopher Alexander refers to as having 'life'.[3]

Keep looking, and the appreciation (or not, if it's bad) may well come to you. When what you see is 'right', you'll feel a little shift in yourself, a sense of anticipation and heightened awareness. Depending on the architecture, it will be followed by appreciation, or joy, or awe, or excitement, or gratitude, or any number of other good feelings. It will happen sooner than you think and can deliver a whole new world of experience to you. At the very least, you can appreciate the skills and intricacies that go into the making of a complex structure. Good architecture makes you feel more alive and can create feelings of warmth and energy. Imagine if pretty much every building you saw made you feel like that. Imagine how much it could enhance your everyday life.

If you succeed in developing your sense of appreciation more keenly, you may experience quite a bit of disappointment, irritation and righteous indignation at many of the buildings you encounter. You may avert your eyes even more than you used to. But that disappointment and irritation was always there. You just didn't know what was causing it. Make no mistake, bad buildings are affecting your health and happiness in more than one way every single day. They're the structural equivalent of a toxic relationship, where the dopamine has drained away and there's an out-of-order sign on the oxytocin dispenser.

Bad buildings create tensions, distress and discord. These negative emotions invade us on a daily basis, they overburden and exhaust us without us even knowing the cause. Conversely, good architecture can energise us, make us feel at one with our surroundings and at peace with ourselves.

You'd be forgiven for thinking the responsibility for this lies on the shoulders of the architect, and at times it does. Architects are like any other profession – not everyone is at the top of their game or where they should be in terms of really understanding the needs of the built environment. And there are those clients who just don't seem to be able to recognise the really good architects when they see them. Either that or they just don't care. But before you send out the lynch mob, you need to know there are a lot of other pressures that can conspire to make your surroundings as dismal as they often are. And your disappointment will be mitigated by your increased pleasure and joy at the architecture that really does work. At the beginning of this book, we mentioned that architecture is the only human endeavour where science and art are so utterly entwined. It takes an architect a long time to become truly accomplished in this complex balancing act. And when they are, it's the skill and artistry that make all the difference, that allow us to experience positive emotions when we look at a building or walk through its door. Given the opportunity, good architects don't design bad buildings. They design buildings that enhance our life and culture, rather than demean it, and they ensure the legacy of our built environment is one worth having. Given the opportunity.

theme one

There's a difference between a building and architecture.

the fantasy architect

Before we talk about the buildings themselves, we'd like you to get to know the people who design them.

The usual fantasy architect is a well-groomed, middle-aged man, smartly dressed in monochrome. Polite and well spoken, he works in a calm and ordered, equally monochrome office, surrounded by computers, models and obliging staff. He exudes an air of quiet confidence. He's a family-orientated man who lives in a stylish home that he's probably designed himself. Professional, articulate and determined in manner, he cares about what he does.

In film, the architect has generally been the go-to good guy. While there are any number of evil doctors, psychopathic scientists, corrupt, greedy lawyers and ruthless businessmen, the architect is the one profession that rarely sees a character as anything other than a clean-cut, perfect romantic lead or reluctant hero with an honourable heart and poetic nature. From Tom Hanks in *Sleepless in Seattle* to Keanu Reeves in *The Lake House*, the architect is usually the man your mother would like you to marry.

The fact that the character is an architect is usually incidental, unless it's Howard Roark in *The Fountainhead* by Ayn Rand, who, many years ago, came to embody a mythical vision of the brooding, uncompromising, obsessive architect on a mission.[1] *The Fountainhead* was published in 1943 and is still in print today. It was followed by a film of the same name a few years later.[2] Gary Cooper played Howard Roark, who some people claim was based on Frank Lloyd Wright. No one could forget the scene where Roark's mentor, who's presumably meant to be a Louis Sullivan figure, lays dying in an ambulance. In a dramatic speech that's part polemic, part personal statement peppered with architectural advice, he delivers the immortal words to Roark: 'I told them, I told them, the form of a building must follow its function.'

Roark became an archetype that persisted for many years: the rugged, lone-wolf architect who's willing to blow up a building because it isn't the way he wants it to be. But eventually, he was superseded by our modern fictional architect who's generally shorthand for a certain kind of guy. He's never shown with stubble and dark patches under his arms after a sweaty all-nighter. Neither is he shown worrying over the cash-flow problems his client's reluctance to pay has created. We never see the look of weary resignation when the developer attempts to cheapen another great design by value engineering. Or the face of thunder when people with little in the way of qualification believe they're competent to do what he does. We never see him locking horns with the project manager.

On television, programmes that follow design and construction, or take us on a tour of interesting buildings, have been popular for many years. They may have occasionally featured architects who are of a different permutation or a little less vanilla, but they rarely dispel our historic fantasy of the archetypal architect.

However, as with all archetypes, there's a dark side. When there's a building-related tragedy, or the public are forced to live with a Brutalist nightmare in their neighbourhood, which architecture students love but everyone else hates, the architect becomes a despised, cackling villain.

In contrast to the stereotype of the male, middle-aged architect, in reality, over 50% of first-year architecture students today are women and they comprise 50% of the under-30 architectural workforce.[3] The numbers for other previously underrepresented groups also continue to improve. However, these changes will take time to filter through to the higher echelons of practice. With a few notable exceptions, the majority of practice owners are men over 40.

Figure 2.2 'The Architect', *The Matrix Reloaded*, Warner Bros, 2003.

Opposite:

Figure 2.1 *The Fountainhead*, Warner Bros, 1949. Howard Roark came to embody a mythical vision of the brooding, uncompromising, obsessive architect.

Around 70% of those practices have fewer than 10 employees; 90% have fewer than 20.[4] They aren't all well spoken by any means, although it's fair to say that after a golden period of social mobility in the latter half of the 20th century, the profession is once again becoming the preserve of the middle classes. And they aren't all mild mannered, either; many an associate has been at the sharp end of a senior architect's temper. It's an open secret that at one well-known practice they've constructed a meeting room with extra acoustic insulation owing to the length and volume of one of the owner's tirades. Nevertheless, while practice owners are as prey to challenges like divorce, drugs and depression as the rest of us, the essence of the fantasy character is often not a million miles away from the truth. But the fantasy of their working lives most certainly is.

There still exist what we might call 'entitled' architects. They come from wealthy backgrounds or marry into them. They usually practise in London, are well connected and seem to hold a disproportionate number of influential positions in architectural organisations like the Royal Institute of British Architects (RIBA). They live with financial certainty from inherited wealth, which allows them the luxury of only entering high-profile competitions and dismissing mundane projects because they don't have to worry about paying the mortgage. Eventually, they win a high-profile scheme, which in turn creates a high-profile practice. That, combined with the fact that they're well connected, assures their success. Things have always been this way and perhaps always will be, but the life of this prominent minority in no way represents the life of the average architect. They are, however, the ones you're most likely to hear about, the ones who have most likely formed your impression of what an architect's life is like. But the truth is, if you find a successful architect from a more modest background, you can be sure they've sweated blood to get where they are.

Architects can be called upon to design anything from a kitchen extension to an airport. It's probably fair to say that the majority of architects would love the opportunity to design a wonderful, one-off building or development, but very few of them get the chance. And like any other profession, while all the architects who are qualified (over 40,000 currently registered in the UK[5]) have a degree of competence, some are much better than others. The standout designs like the Gherkin in London, designed by Norman Foster, or the Metropol Parasol in Seville, designed by Jürgen Mayer, are like the catwalk of architecture. Generally, it's a few architectural equivalents of Vera Wang or Stella McCartney who get to display their wares in such a dramatic manner. And as with fashion, they set the potential for high-street adaptations. Buildings can span high end to bargain basement.

It takes seven years to qualify as an architect, the same length of time it takes to qualify as a medical doctor. It's several years more before architects are allowed to be responsible for the design of a complex project, which is akin to the medical doctor becoming a consultant. After that, they may take a senior position in the practice they work for, or start their own. When we think of a medical doctor, we often think of them as simply caring for their patients. We don't necessarily picture them attending meetings and seminars, teaching and assessing, filling in forms and attending to administration, trying to do their best on inadequate budgets. Likewise, we often only think of the architect creating a design for a building then keeping an eye on it. Architects are involved in the planning process, meetings, health and safety, environmental and legal obligations, procurement, value engineering, teaching, professional development and many other ongoing issues. Practice owners are running a business, they have staff to consider, rent and bills to pay. Like most of us, they don't necessarily get to do the

27

things they'd like to do, and often work over 60 hours a week. Like most of us, they have to make a living and are sometimes forced to make compromises they'd really rather not make.

Architects' offices tend to be relatively muted, with a slightly religious atmosphere, as if there's a sleeping dragon under the floor that everyone's quite keen not to wake up. Architecture is something of a cult in its own way, a siblinghood of devout practitioners, like any group of people who've shared the same baptisms of fire. Along with their many other modern skills, practice owners do sometimes have a touch of Howard Roark, being brooding, intense and charismatic figures whose presence can be quietly intimidating. As you might expect, architects don't see the built environment the same way others do. They're concerned with things like proportions, details, materials, measurements, loadbearing, scale and massing. They know about stuff like rain-screen cladding, chamfers, elevations and junctions. They're wise to who nicked an idea from Otto Wagner or Frank Gehry. And the really good ones experience bad buildings as pain. We can only speculate on what that encyclopaedic knowledge of technical and creative considerations has done to their brains. After seven years of training and many more of seriously hard graft, the average architect's salary is less than half that of the average doctor's. So much for the fantasy. Architects don't enjoy the status in society that doctors often do. Perhaps somewhere down the line you'll decide whether they should.

Figure 2.3 The Metropol
Parasol, Seville, by
Jürgen Mayer, 2011.
A beautiful example of
high-profile architecture.

theme two

Becoming a good architect
is a tough gig.

too many
cooks spoil
the broth

A high-end chain of sandwich shops wants to create a new flagship sandwich. The owners hire a celebrated chef to create a recipe for the sandwich. The chef creates the recipe, which is approved by the owners. The owners then put the production of the sandwich out to tender, accepting the lowest bid. But then the company that won the tender finds it can't actually make the sandwich for the price it quoted; the time it takes to make the sandwich is much longer than originally estimated and the ingredients are too expensive. To fulfil the contract and in an effort to make some profit, the company calls upon a sous chef it routinely employs, who uses cheaper ingredients and takes less care about how the sandwich is presented, despite the original chef's protestations. In the end, the sandwich bears little resemblance to the chef's original vision. The chef is disappointed to have their name associated with it and displeased that being replaced by another chef has resulted in them being paid less. The owners of the sandwich shop chain are disappointed because the sandwich is an inferior product and doesn't sell well, which in turn means disappointed customers, many of whom take their business elsewhere. The production company is disappointed because it's barely made any profit.

It may surprise you to learn this is a regular occurrence in the construction industry. The sandwich shop chain owners are the client, the original chef is the architect and the production company is the contractor.

The process by which a building project is set in motion is known as procurement. There are many kinds of procurement: indeed, it would be possible to write a whole book about the subject. If you're thrilled by complicated procedures, guidelines, laws and contracts, it would be a good read for you. One kind of procurement is known as 'Design and Build', a common process by which buildings are constructed at the present time. Design and Build contracts gained popularity in the 1990s and were seen as a magic bullet to solve the risk of projects going over time and over budget, not that the majority of them did in any significant sense. It's always the major projects that skyrocket in the most dramatic manner that the public generally hears about, or the over-optimistic and inexperienced one-off house aspirants on Channel 4's *Grand Designs*.

At its most damaging extreme, imagine the architect has been awarded a contract to design a low-rise office complex in a medium sized UK city by their client. They design the building, and it passes planning. The project is put out to tender for a contractor to construct the building. So far, so good. Actually, this is often as good as it gets. At this stage, the architect can be novated to the contractor, which basically means the contractor now 'owns' them. The contractor is in a powerful position and may seek to prevent the architect from having any contact with the client and from engaging in the crucially important site visits that will ensure all is going according to plan. The contractor is also in a position to make it difficult for the architect to fight for the integrity of the project. This process might be taken further, when our architect becomes designated as the concept or planning architect. The contractor then employs a delivery architect as they go through a process called value engineering, which sounds much cooler than it actually is. It's basically a cost-cutting exercise. Value engineering isn't a bad thing per se: in the right hands, it can be an effective process of collaboration to assess whether savings can be made without any loss of quality, safety or longevity. Goldsmith Street in Norwich is a great example of positive value engineering, where the client, Norwich City Council, allowed the architect to take control of the process, ensuring the preservation of design quality and important features, while saving significant amounts of money. The development won the RIBA Stirling Prize in 2019, a stunning achievement for a social housing project.

Value engineering can also rescue a project in unforeseen circumstances, such as a rapid increase in the cost of materials. However, in an all-too-common scenario, the contractor has pitched their price too low in order to get the contract. In an attempt to make a profit, they value engineer: they cheapen anything on the project they possibly can. To do this, they use the delivery architect who's employed by them. The delivery architect is seen as a more technical and safer option in terms of cost cutting than the concept architect, but they can't possibly feel the same level of passion and vision about the project. The delivery architect, of necessity, cares more about what the contractor wants than fidelity to the planning architect's vision. They won't have the same concerns about the quality of the original design. A similar scenario would be if, a little way into the final of the BBC's *MasterChef*, the competitors preparing their gourmet dinner were forced to leave the kitchen while the meal was finished by a contract caterer armed with inferior ingredients. In reality, concept architects are wise to this and will often design in a way that's hard to cheapen or will make things a little more expensive than they expect the outcome to be. Nevertheless, whether it succeeds or fails, the value engineering process will seek to cheapen everything that doesn't contravene the original planning approval. If our concept architect continues to make waves as they fight for the project, they may get a reputation for being 'difficult' and risk losing work in the future. Compliant delivery architects are a growth area and often end up making more money than the concept architects. In the end, such buildings are not what they were meant to be.

Figure 3.1 Goldsmith Street, Norwich, by Mikhail Riches, 2019. The social housing project won the RIBA Stirling Prize.

The client finds a Design and Build contract appealing because the price is fixed and therefore entails less financial risk, but they are often disappointed with the results. They asked for a Land Rover Defender and ended up getting a transit van. Design and Build can be a race to the bottom and is one of the factors in why many of the buildings you see are so disappointing. Value engineering can exert a profound effect on the look and feel of a building. It frequently flattens surfaces, so they're much less aesthetically pleasing and interesting. The cheapening of materials, unsurprisingly, also takes its toll. For instance, there can be a world of difference between cheap brick and quality brick, which not only affects the pleasure of the eye in terms of tone and texture, but also diminishes lifespan.

That's all bad enough, but it gets much, much worse.

In the early hours of 14 June 2017, a fire spread through Grenfell Tower. Seventy-one people died, many homes were destroyed and countless lives have been affected. The fire appeared to be accelerated by the building's exterior cladding system, leading to a national programme of extensive testing of the cladding on other high-rise buildings. This revealed widespread use of aluminium composite materials, which did not meet the limited combustibility requirements of building regulations guidance, and raised concerns for the safety of others … This tragic incident should not have happened in our country in the 21st century. We now all have the opportunity to respond in a way that will lead to lasting change that makes people safer in the future.

DAME JUDITH HACKITT[1]

Whilst the events leading to the Grenfell Tragedy were complex and manifold, value engineering was a contributing factor. As yet, we don't know what other events may lie in wait for us. It's possible that there are hundreds or even thousands of buildings out there with potentially serious or even deadly problems.

A plethora of reports, inquiries, speeches, lectures, articles, recommendations and guidelines have called for procurement to change. Some local authorities have agreed the original architect should be the one who sees the project through to completion but, as far as we're aware, none have taken the client and/ or developer to task when it doesn't happen. Design and Build has been the status quo for so long that people have stopped believing it could be any other way. Indeed, younger clients often aren't aware of how a single architect would once be in control from inception to completion. This safeguarded the notion of 'the golden thread', a single point of continuity and responsibility from first sketch to end result. The golden thread needs to be protected because it, in turn, protects the project on every level, from fidelity to the original vision to issues of building safety. In the current system where everyone is mitigating risk, it's all too easy for no one to take responsibility.

These themes were significant features of the government-commissioned *Hackitt Report*, officially known as *The Independent Review of Building Regulations and Fire Safety*, a final version of which was published in 2018.[2] It established a clear and comprehensive set of guidelines for the construction industry to ensure that tragic events such as Grenfell could never happen again. Within those guidelines, it draws attention to the importance of maintaining a golden thread and states that

Figure 3.2 Grenfell Tower, London, 2017. Value engineering was a contributing factor in the complex event cascade that led to this terrible tragedy.

procurement practices that can lead to poor design and safety standards need to be addressed. The report states:

> A lack of clear roles and responsibilities, and ambiguous regulations and guidance allow the market to procure without building safety in mind; there is no requirement or incentive to do so. Alongside this, unhelpful behaviours such as contract terms and payment practices, which prioritise speed and low cost solutions, exacerbate this situation. These characteristics provide poor value for money and poor building safety outcomes.[3]

In Chapter One we described the difference between a building and architecture; how Delight is what turns a building into architecture. How functions and structural elements have to be synthesised to create it, the same way a composer synthesises any number of sounds to create a beautiful symphony. If we take the beautiful symphony and remove just one of its themes, the music changes and not for the better. Remove too many and the symphony can become a cacophony – and, in the context of architecture, a dangerous cacophony at that.

Until we recognise that the best person to be in the heart of the process is the original, experienced architect, chances are our built environment will simply get worse, not only in terms of beauty, but also safety and longevity. Procurement is a major factor in why so many of our buildings are letting us down.

theme three

Let the architect be the architect.

the history lesson

We learn from history that we do not learn from history.
GEORG HEGEL, PHILOSOPHER[1]

The history of architecture is also the history of trends. Architecture is no more immune to fashion than any other field of human endeavour.

When we're in the midst of a trend, whether philosophical or practical, we often think it's a great thing, the final solution, the bee's knees. It's only later that we might consider the trend wasn't quite what we thought it was and reflect upon the influences that brought this state to bear upon us. Fashion often seems most cool when only a few people are doing it. Then everyone joins in and it becomes a cliché and doesn't seem quite so cool anymore. If you suggested to the average architect that they're as prey to fashion as anyone else when it comes to designing, they might well react with some incredulity. But the evidence is there and can't be denied. The fact is, we don't always consciously know how fashion driven we are.

The roots of fashion lie in instinctive behaviour. Our closest relatives, chimpanzees and bonobos, understand fashion very well.[2] If a high-ranking member of the group does something new, the rest usually follow suit. This makes perfect sense in evolutionary terms; if the trendsetter has risen to the top or near it, mimicking their behaviour might well be a good strategy for success. Human primates have taken this instinct and raised it to a whole other level, as we do with so many things. The (unconscious) desire to be accepted can also be a motivating factor in following the latest trends, or equally, as a trendsetter, the desire to stand out. None of these matters are trivial or irrelevant; without the drive to embrace the new, nothing would ever progress and the truly useful ideas and innovations would never be discovered. Unfortunately, the kernel tends to come with a great deal of shell that needs to be discarded. This isn't too much of a problem with a piece of clothing or the latest thing in fine dining – both are short lived and easily disposed of. But when it comes to a building, it will generally be with us for a very long time and if it isn't, it's expensive, cumbersome and very wasteful to remove. A knotty problem indeed.

The pressure on architects to adopt a particular style starts when they're students. The students are taught by lecturers who may have their own intellectual and philosophical fashion and design agendas, which, as one might expect, often influence their students. Whatever the lecturers' tastes and opinions, they're unlikely to include anything 'traditional' or ornate, which will often be labelled as pastiche. Once the students graduate, the situation can become further compounded by peer pressure, the philosophy of the practice they work in and the wishes of the client and developer. Understandably, clients and developers don't want to lose money. Unless it's a flagship building, the client and/or developer is likely to ask for a design like something else they've seen or previously built because that's considered to be the safest option.

The problem with fashionable agendas is that if they stick around long enough and are adopted by enough people, they start to get treated as though they're a truth rather than an opinion. Until the next one comes along.

From the turn of the 20th century, there's been a progression through various stages of architecture in Britain, although timelines can be deceptive. Just because a particular style may have been prominent, it doesn't mean everything built during that period was of that style. Also, styles feed off and feed into each other; the shift tends to be more gradual than we might think it is. New techniques

Figures 4.1a and 4.1b Castle Ward, County Down, Northern Ireland, architect unknown, possibly James Bridges. The curious case of the 18th-century Castle Ward demonstrates different styles existing in the same timeframe. Owing to the contrasting tastes of Lord Bangor and his wife, Lady Ann Bligh, one half of the house is Palladian and the other Georgian Gothic.

and materials also enable a style to develop. You'll note a lack of 18th-century tower blocks because the technology to create them didn't exist at the time.

Here's a whistle-stop tour through the prevalent trends of the past 150 or so years.

The Arts and Crafts Movement (approximately 1880 to 1920) was a response to its supporters' belief that mass production and mechanisation was leading to a decline in standards, that industrial architecture was ugly and inhuman and that past styles had more to do with pretension than what people needed in their homes. It was closely allied with the philosophy of the Art Workers' Guild, founded by John Ruskin and William Morris, whose designs for wallpaper and furnishings remain popular to this day. In terms of architecture, it promoted the principles of clarity, variety, asymmetry and traditional construction using local materials. The Arts and Crafts Movement set great store by craft and simplicity. In terms of both style and quality, Arts and Crafts was very successful, and its buildings are still valued.

Art Nouveau developed from the Arts and Crafts Movement and existed contemporaneously (1883 to 1914). Greatly influenced by the natural world, it was defined by organic shapes, sinuous lines, arches, curves and sensual ornamentation. It was inspired by the

Figure 4.2 Oriel Chambers, Liverpool, by Peter Ellis, 1864. A precursor to the modern tower and the first use of curtain walling with a cast-iron frame in England.

Following pages:

Figure 4.3 *The Century is Over. Evolutionary Tree of 20th-Century Architecture*, by Charles Jencks, 2000.

Evolutionary Tree 2000, Charles Jencks, no copyright

Figure 4.4 29 Avenue
Rapp, Paris, by Jules
Lavirotte, 1901,
photographed in
1972. An example of
Art Nouveau.

desire to break with tradition and explore newer, freer forms of visual expression. Its influence was strongest in cities, where it was used most widely for the design of upper-class homes and buildings such as hotels. Some of you have perhaps enjoyed time in the Willow Tea Rooms in Glasgow or taken a selfie outside an Art Nouveau Metro station in Paris. You may have joined the Barcelona crowds in enjoying the work of Antoni Gaudí. Art Nouveau remains a loved and popular style that came to an abrupt halt in the UK at the onset of the First World War. It was more important than its relatively short period of favour suggests, as it made a decisive break from the forms and revivals, which dominated previous decades.

Art Deco emerged following the First World War, in what were known as the Roaring Twenties. This movement was characterised by sleek, linear geometric forms arranged and broken up by curved ornamental elements. Decorative glass was big in Art Deco, as were highly stylised interiors. Art Deco cinemas appeared in many UK towns and cities as a trip to the 'pictures' became a popular pastime and although many have been demolished, some are still with us, either as independent cinemas or repurposed buildings.
It was also a popular form for commerce, as industrialists found the style easily transferable from package design to architecture. Art Deco, too, became a casualty of war.

It's perhaps difficult for us to truly imagine the havoc that the Second World War wreaked on the built environment. Vast numbers of houses in the UK were destroyed by bombing, with many more badly damaged. When other types of buildings are entered into the equation, it created formidable problems in terms of regeneration. Enter Modernism. The Modernist Movement had been growing in popularity in Europe for many years, although it hadn't achieved much prominence in Britain. Modernism believed that form should

follow function, that the building's purpose should be the starting point for its design, rather than aesthetic considerations. It was a rational, analytical, utilitarian philosophy that embraced the minimalist and rejected ornament. Modernism's ambitions were also largely humanitarian, as within the movement there was a genuine belief that it could make the world a better place. The new methods of construction – such as steel and concrete frames, advances in window technology and craned-in panelised systems – meant buildings such as prefabricated houses could be completed with speed and ease. This proved to be an urgently required sticking plaster over the country's structural wounds and easily aligned with the Modernist aesthetic.

Modernist buildings abound and don't always have a good name. They're generally described as compositions comprised of geometrical forms, often with flat roofs. An emphasis is placed on horizontal lines, reinforced concrete, steel frames, curtain walls and ribbon windows. There's minimal or no ornamentation, a white or neutral palette, with light, spacious, open-plan interiors. In the next couple of chapters, we'll be discussing some of the catastrophic errors made by some of the authorities, architects and developers looking for a quick fix and a brave new world in terms of housing, which they believed Modernism could provide. That's without getting on to the dozens of shopping centres and commercial buildings that enjoyed a shockingly short shelf life.

Figure 4.5 Royal Institute of British Architects, 66 Portland Place, London, by George Grey Wornum, 1934. An example of Art Deco.

It wouldn't be unreasonable to say that post-war Modernism became something of a religion for many in the architectural community. Perhaps even a cult. At its heart was a rather naive but well-meaning belief it could lead to a kind of utopia. And while opinions differ, there can be little doubt that Modernism created a vast and complex web of influence over building design.

Modernism frequently offers a sharp divide between for and against. Modernist buildings helped to reconstruct many towns and cities after the Second World War. Modernism also ultimately laid waste to some of these towns and cities. Modernism allowed the creation of new structural forms, many of them beautiful and engaging. It also murdered millennia of decorative tradition. Modernism enabled the creation of bright, open-plan spaces. It also hardened the landscape with flat steel-and-glass surfaces. At the end of the day, there's much to praise and much to criticise.

Frank Lloyd Wright is perhaps the most-loved Modernist architect and his buildings, especially his houses, are so highly valued that they regularly feature in films, including *Blade Runner, Grand Canyon, The Aviator, Gattaca* and *Men in Black*. He was also the inspiration for sets in *Game of Thrones* and the series remake of *Westworld*. Quite remarkable considering most of his work was created in the first half of the 20th century.

Come the 1980s, Post-Modernism was starting to leave its mark. Whereas Modernism was devoted to simplicity and order, Post-Modernism embraced complexity and contradiction. Modernist architecture had been repeatedly criticised for its rigid doctrines, uniformity and lack of local and cultural context. The Post-Modernists wanted to achieve a more democratic form of accessible architecture. It was something of a free-for-all, drawing on every architectural style and period with idiosyncratic, rule-breaking forms. Post-Modernism is

Figure 4.6 The Ennis House, Los Angeles, by Frank Lloyd Wright, 1924. The house featured in the 1982 science-fiction film *Bladerunner,* which was set in 2019.

55

known for bright colours, playfulness, variety in materials and shapes and classical motifs. Perhaps the most famous Post-Modernist building in the UK is the MI6 building in London (1994), designed by Terry Farrell and Partners, along with the famous (or infamous) TV-AM Building (1998), which has now been listed.

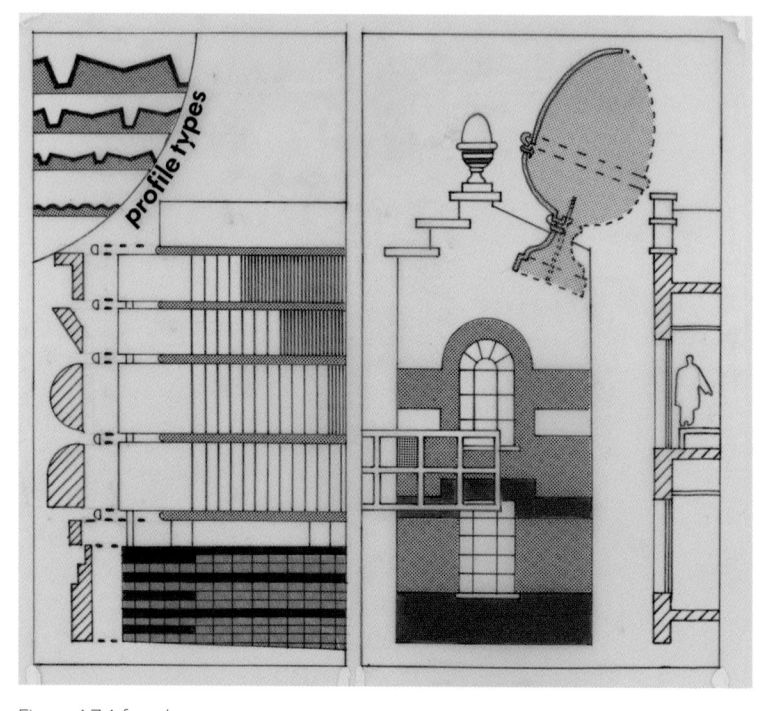

Figure 4.7 A façade study of the Post-Modernist TV-AM Building, London, by Terry Farrell, 1998.

Opposite:

Figure 4.8 Another example of Post-Modernism – James Stirling's final building, No.1 Poultry, City of London, 1998.

However, Post-Modernism didn't completely draw a line under Modernism. Modernism's two most important mantras, *form follows function* and *less is more*, haven't quite left the premises. They're still hanging around like those drunken guests who don't seem to realise the party ended a couple of hours ago. These were statements that aligned to Adolf Loos's influential 1910 lecture 'Ornament and Crime', which was subsequently published in various languages over the next few years. Essentially, Loos considered ornament to be a sign of primitive culture and that it caused buildings to be unfashionable sooner than they needed to be; the time, effort and cost involved in its creation was a crime. It distracted from the function of the object and the money spent on ornamentation could be better used for the public good. Smooth surfaces and universality were the solution. Le Corbusier picked up this idea and ran with it. The rest is Modernist history. Despite being in a post-modern age, there are still many architects who feel decidedly nervous about the whole idea of ornament. Folks, ornament is not a crime. Far from it. Bad design, on the other hand …

We can see that the fashions of architecture have, to some extent, reflected society at any given time. Arts and Crafts was a response to the rampage of industrialisation and the fears and doubts many people experienced about this seismic shift. Art Nouveau reflected the beginnings of liberation from sensual and artistic repression into more bohemian and free-thinking modes of living. Art Deco was a kind of halfway house between Art Nouveau and Modernism; not quite rejecting the curves and decoration, but seeking a sleeker, more technological feel, which reflected the expansion of showy corporate wealth and increasing industry. Modernism displayed a full engagement with the machine age, where there was a belief that science and functionality could create a utopia. And while Modernism had an ideal, Post-Modernism reflected the loss of an ideal.

Figure 4.9 Steiner House,
Vienna, by Adolf Loos,
1910. The original –
some might say bland –
Modernist building.

Currently, there's no obvious trend, at least not one we can recognise at this moment in time. But all too often in commercial buildings, 'Modernist style' or 'minimal' has become a convenient excuse for producing cheap, shoddy and badly designed buildings, while many – often poor-quality – modern housing developments hark back to previous styles such as Georgian or Edwardian, with pitched roofs, visible chimneys and other characteristic stylings.

Ultimately, there's one single, compelling message. It's generally only the most durable, adaptable, well-designed and well-built examples of all these stages that we're left with in the fullness of time. Only architecture of usefulness, quality and beauty persists. So the question arises, when we're in the midst of a style, trend or movement, how can we ensure what's built will stand the test of time?

This is an important question because 50,000 buildings are demolished in the UK every year, which is a landfill headache whichever way you slice it.[3] There's no doubt that a reasonable proportion of them are asking for it, but given the current need to provide sustainable solutions in our built environment, this figure should be improved upon. The most sustainable thing we can possibly do is to reimagine and repurpose those buildings we can save and ensure the new ones we create will still be standing, usable, adaptable, loved and appreciated in hundreds of years. It's a little depressing to speculate on how many buildings being constructed in the current era will fit that bill.

Figures 4.10a and 4.10b The Old School House, Bolton, Greater Manchester, by Nick Moss Architects, 2023. This building could easily have been a candidate for demolition (4.10a). Instead, new life that's sympathetic to the old has been infused into a badly neglected location. The repurposing of the building into accommodation has extended its life far into the future (4.10b).

61

The history of architecture spans thousands of years and in light of this, perhaps there's another way we might look at things. Every building that's gone before us is evidence. Evidence of what works and what doesn't; evidence of what always works and evidence of what never works. We might consider paying closer attention to the universal themes that present themselves to us and synthesise them into forms that are satisfying and beautiful. Architecture that has the courage to shed cultish beliefs and embrace eternal qualities need be no less innovative and creative than anything that's gone before. This is the kind of architecture that can and will enrich our lives and impoverish our landfill. All the clues are contained in the history of humankind. If we take the trouble to listen, we just might hear them calling to us.

Architecture should speak of its time
and place but yearn for timelessness.
FRANK GEHRY, ARCHITECT[4]

theme four

Good architecture is a joy forever.

the white heat of technology

When we think of architecture in a historical context, it's often grand buildings such as temples and mosques, palaces and great halls that come to mind. But this concentration on the grand may cause us to forget that for most of our history the majority of the population lived in accommodation that was barely fit for purpose. This fact is easily overlooked because while the grand is often still with us, the squalid and unfit was demolished long ago or fell down of its own accord. In the newly emerging towns and cities of the Industrial Revolution, the squalid and unfit intensified and abounded. The privations, sickness and mortality rates created by these poor housing conditions was well documented, perhaps most famously by Friedrich Engels.[1] A city such as Manchester is still in possession of its imposing neo-Gothic Town Hall, designed by Alfred Waterhouse and completed in 1877. The jerry-built slums in the vicinity that existed for workers during the many years before and after its construction are long gone.

The housing that bucked this trend is noteworthy, not least developments such as Port Sunlight in Merseyside, a valiant and successful 19th-century attempt to provide the working classes with decent living conditions. This combination of model industrial housing with the landscape and architectural values of the garden suburb has proved to possess longevity. Today it's both listed and highly prized. By the turn of the 20th century, along with increasing socio-political pressure, developments like Port Sunlight, Saltaire in Shipley, West Yorkshire, and Bournville in Birmingham, commissioned by their factory owners, had already sown the seeds of change. Unfortunately, two world wars and a deep economic depression in between them meant that the seeds took a long time to grow. It wasn't until the latter half of the 20th century that the majority of the UK population began to enjoy decent housing. But within this much-needed attempt to raise the living standards of the

Figure 5.1 Manchester slums, 1908.

population lies a cautionary tale that demonstrates the importance of taking human instinct and sensibilities into account when approaching design.

In 1963, the leader of the Labour Party, Harold Wilson, who would become Prime Minister the following year, delivered his seminal 'White Heat of Technology' speech, claiming that a new Britain would be forged by a scientific revolution, a revolution that would finally allow the population to achieve living standards that had previously been enjoyed by only a small, privileged minority. The speech was well received and it was in this atmosphere of enthusiasm for the optimistic, new and transformative that a Labour Government was elected in 1964.[2]

As the 1960s started to famously 'swing' with innovations such as transistor radios, early computers and the contraceptive pill, there was still plenty of work to be done in terms of the conditions in which people lived. To relieve the chronic housing shortage and lingering slum conditions, the mass building of council accommodation was a necessary and well-meaning solution to unfit circumstances. And Modernism, combined with new building technologies as described in the previous chapter, appealed to many as the perfect, progressive 'white heat' answer to the problem.

In the early half of the 20th century, Modernism was largely the preserve of wealthy individuals who could afford to build expensive, one-off houses, but in post-Second World War Britain, it became an epidemic, not least in these abundant council accommodation projects of the 1960s. Unlike many European countries, apartment

Figure 5.2 Robin Hood Gardens, Poplar, London, by Alison and Peter Smithson, 1972.

living had never been a major feature of British working-class life. Despite the fact that any number of surveys indicated it wasn't what people wanted, that was about to change.[3]

The new Modernist model promoted what would be a new way of living. Well-spaced, high-rise accommodation providing plentiful daylight would be connected by 'streets in the sky'. These 'streets in the sky' were substantial deck access projects where the dwellings were lifted from the ground into the air and stacked along elevated walkways. The idea was that these 'streets' would inspire social interaction while the common areas could be used as parkland. And according to the Modernist aesthetic, they were 'rational', minimalist and eschewed any form of decoration.

This model was based on the assumption that the housing could dictate the culture, rather than the culture dictating the housing, a model firmly – and in retrospect, naively – embraced by the government and local authorities, planners, developers and some architects. Once the masses were safely installed and stored in their homes they would cheerfully and politely go about their business, socialise on the walkways and have family picnics in the parkland, happy and grateful in their new way of life. It seems the powers that be and architects such as Peter and Alison Smithson, who were popular choices for this kind of development, didn't fully appreciate the force of the cultural glue that had previously held working-class areas together, the same way that architect Berthold Lubetkin didn't appreciate that penguins wouldn't actually like the Modernist penguin pool he designed for London Zoo. The pool, completed in 1934, left the penguins unable to burrow, which was part of their courting ritual, and the concrete gave them aching joints. They vacated the premises in 2004, to be replaced by Chinese alligators who proved to be equally unenthusiastic about their surroundings.[4]

Figure 5.3 The
Modernist penguin
pool at London Zoo, by
Berthold Lubetkin, 1934.
It wasn't exactly a hit
with the penguins.

In terms of housing, too many of those involved assumed they knew what was best for the people who would ultimately inhabit these developments. And the people who had so looked forward to the excitement of a new home that was dry and offered plentiful daylight, storage, indoor plumbing and running hot water could not have known of the catastrophe that was about to unfold.

The casual observer from a higher social echelon may only have noticed factors such as overcrowding and snotty-nosed kids, broken prams and brassy brawls in the slum neighbourhoods set for demolition. But beneath the obvious privations and poor conditions in the areas to be rehoused, a self-regulating system had existed for many years. These were geographical communities that relied upon the close proximity of family members, where everyone could see what everyone else was doing and families in the street knew the measure of each other. Communities where the older men did their best to make sure that the young or delinquent didn't get out of hand. Children played outside under the watchful eyes of their mothers through the window. These were streets where people could simply step outside their front door to watch the church Whitsuntide parade. Where small enterprises could emerge organically and word of mouth was easy to achieve. Yards and allotments allowed connection to nature and additional resources through the growing of flowers, fruit and vegetables. The system in which life took place had developed over time as a natural response to the needs and circumstances of those communities. While the old houses crumbled, the culture remained intact.

Unfortunately, the new deck access projects didn't work as traditional streets, with their blank front doors on one side and sizeable drops on the other. In reality, there was no street life and nobody across the 'street' who could keep an eye on the other side.

Walking from home to a lift or stairwell could be quite intimidating. Without the watchful eyes of a neighbourhood, these lifts and stairwells became magnets for those of disruptive or criminal intention. And for the majority of tenants, who rightly or wrongly had no appreciation for this new aesthetic, the featureless, utilitarian design they couldn't alter made them feel like they were living in a prison, rather than a home. Even the parkland didn't work, however well meaning.

The idea of the high-rise based in parkland is credited to Le Corbusier. Le Corbusier's ambitions were broadly humanitarian, giving people all the light, air and green space they'd been so deprived of in previous decades. What could go wrong? What went wrong is a complete lack of understanding with regard to human instincts, most specifically those of protection and territory. People generally don't like being overlooked, especially when they're suddenly thrust into the alien experience of being overlooked from a great height by literally hundreds of strangers. When most people are in a position to do so, buying a home that isn't overlooked is usually quite high on their agenda. As is private outside space, rather than space that isn't enclosed and not owned by any specific person. Such is the power of our territorial instincts. These factors created a sense of vulnerability that residents found – given their previous culture and sensibilities – impossible to overcome, and rather than liberating them, added to their sense of imprisonment.

Form follows function is all very well. The problem is that you have to be aware of all the functions. Too many crucial, immutable functions weren't factored into these developments, like community, neighbourhood, tradition, familiarity, instincts, defensible and private space, not to mention human scale. And to most of the general public, the idea that decoration doesn't serve a function is ludicrous.

Projects that had a greater reliance on housing and where communities were moved together and therefore remained intact were much more successful. Within three decades, most of the 'streets in the sky' were irredeemable and ended up being demolished.[5] Without the glue that had previously held them together, and with nothing to replace it, the communities simply fell apart. And the accommodation itself was often poorly built, creating constant and expensive headaches.

Rather than these environments serving as a positive force in people's lives, instead they became a negative one. Problems such as disadvantage, isolation, family breakdown, social difficulties and sometimes poor management were severely aggravated by the housing itself. And once the deterioration became endemic, how muted might the hopes and dreams, the creativity and ambition of the people who were trapped within them have become? The difference we feel in our wellbeing, especially our sense of hope, when we're in a positive and life-affirming environment, compared to an oppressive, neglected and ugly one, is worthy of recognition.

How uplifting might those developments have been if those involved had opened their hearts and minds, immersed themselves in the daily lives of the people and addressed genuine desires and needs that would have become readily apparent. If they'd done so, this would be a very different story. How much less demolition, disruption and further rehousing could have been avoided with a little less naivety regarding human need. Once it was over, the eternal qualities became apparent: the desire for connectedness, the hard-wired instincts about what is satisfying and what allows a community to thrive. Mess with these at your peril. 'Streets in the sky' is a sad illustration of where fashionable and well-meaning but incomplete philosophies can lead, but we view it with the wisdom of hindsight. The social experiment was costly, both in monetary terms and the lives of the people who were stuck in the middle of it. Two good reasons to make sure its results are burned upon our consciousness forever.

After this episode, the idea of tenant participation began to establish itself. The notorious Hulme Crescents in Manchester, built in 1972, was the largest housing development in Europe, containing 3,284 deck-access homes, which turned out to have serious design and construction errors. Hulme was demolished in 1993, just 21 years after it was constructed. Ironically, each of the Crescents was named after a distinguished architect. Hulme was redesigned by a number of different architects in the 1990s after a comprehensive process of tenant consultation. And guess what the tenants wanted? A low-rise development of mainly houses (see also Figure 10.1). And if 21 years seems like an appallingly short lifespan, consider the 1977 Southgate Housing development in Runcorn, designed by James Stirling. Southgate comes in at just nine years.

Nevertheless, it's important to remember that a notable proportion of the various players, including architects, weren't on board with the doomed developments; indeed, at a later date, they often became the cavalry riding in to save the day. And many of the more timelessly designed housing schemes that were constructed during this period proved to be a haven of vastly improved facilities for their tenants and matured into stable communities. Unlike 'streets in the sky', they were the seeds that didn't fall on stony ground.

Deck access itself need not be put in the stocks. The developments we've described took place within a particular set of circumstances. What was fundamentally a scorched-earth policy meant that residents could not return to their previous way of life, but instead had no choice but to endure the anomic conditions they suddenly found themselves in. These developments also proved wholly

Figure 5.4 The notorious Hulme Crescents, Manchester, by Hugh Wilson and J. L. Womersley, 1972.

Figure 5.5 Southgate
Housing, Runcorn, by
James Stirling, 1977.
The development had a
lifespan of just nine years.

unsuitable for families with young children, were too large scale and often poorly built. Deck access became structure *non grata* for many years and has only recently begun to re-emerge. It's an effective antidote to single-aspect, deep-plan apartments, which can suffer from poor levels of daylight and ventilation. Sensitively designed deck access can provide dual-aspect homes in a high-density development and grant each home a 'fresh air' front door. It provides cross-air ventilation, daylight on both sides and a variation in outlook. The demands of modern building regulations are increasingly encouraging architects to use this layout. And a well-planned scheme can yield around 300 homes per hectare. All worthwhile reasons to suggest we shouldn't throw the baby out with the bathwater.

So, what are we to learn from this 20th-century snapshot where the new broom believed it could sweep clean? That longevity and satisfaction in housing requires due diligence with regard to instinct, culture and beauty. Nevertheless, this should not imply a slavish copying of previous successes. While the architect needs to be sensitive to the community, they can't become its servant. Great architecture includes innovation and the courage of the new. There's a balance to be struck between eternal qualities and contemporary designs. Today, there are many examples of architects, such as Peter Barber, designing modern housing that's beautiful and sensitive. The modern vernacular philosophy, where housing design takes account of history, environment and the needs of its inhabitants, generally works well for everyone, but all too often this type of housing project is small, expensive and based in London. In a country where there are housing shortages in many sectors, people will take what they can get, but that doesn't mean what they can get is what they deserve. It's a situation that by no means lies only on the shoulders of the architect.

Figure 5.6 Park Hill, Sheffield, originally designed by Jack Lynn and Ivor Smith and opened in 1961, has been revitalised by architects Hawkins\Brown, Studio Egret West and Mikhail Riches for developer Urban Splash. One of the original 'streets in the sky' has found a new lease of life.

It would be easy to assume the story has reached its natural conclusion. Today, most (but by no means all) of the population enjoys decent standards of housing in the functional sense. But the evidence we do not live by bread alone is glaringly apparent in this cautionary tale. If 'streets in the sky' was the migraine, much of the current housing in this country is a dull ache behind the eyes in terms of optimising the satisfaction of human need beyond its most basic, functional aspects. For instance, none of the major housebuilders routinely use architects to design individual developments. They have a number of predesigned property types, they decide where they're going to be placed on a plot and that's that. All too often, they're a superficial and listless reference to previous eras. These properties are generally mediocre and uninspiring, the development patterns dissatisfying, but people are going to buy them, give them love and do their best for them because it's all they have to work with. There's no doubt it works as a business strategy, but it doesn't do much in terms of beauty, emotional satisfaction or architectural legacy. We're not in 'streets in the sky' territory anymore, but we're certainly a long way from optimum living conditions. Employing the services of an architect who can produce designs of delight and fight for the integrity of the scheme would greatly benefit the quality of our accommodation and make little dent in the profit margins. A talented architect can bring life to a project that allows an area to flourish in the best sense of the word. It's a shame that nowadays an architect is more likely to be called upon to create or reimagine a unique social housing project than stock for private sale.

Figure 5.7 Hortsley, Seaford, by architects RCKa, 2018. How deck access becomes integral to retirement living.

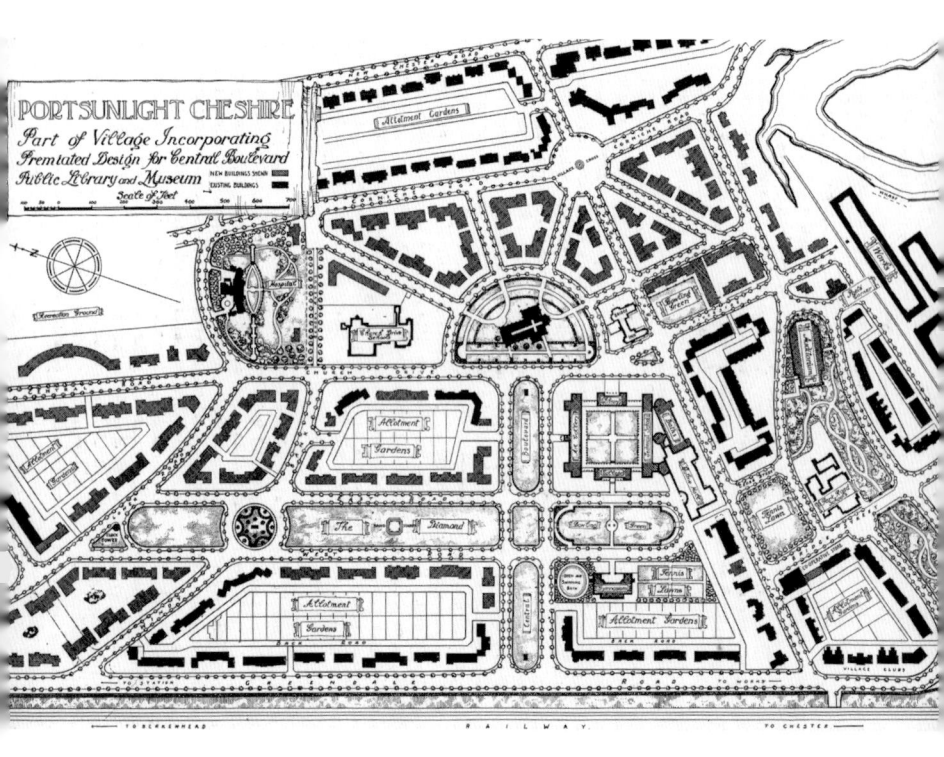

Figure 5.8 Competition
design for Port Sunlight,
Merseyside, showing the
central boulevard, public
library and museum.
The late 19th-century
village, which was a new
approach to workers'
housing, contains more
than 900 Grade II listed
buildings.

At this point we come full circle and return to Port Sunlight, Merseyside, built by the Lever Brothers in the late 19th century to house their workforce. Within this remarkable development, each block of houses was designed by a different architect. Currently, it contains more than 900 Grade II listed buildings and large numbers of people go to see it every year. It doesn't take a genius to work out that if it weren't for the skill and vision of those architects and the profound understanding of the way people live best, visitors and listings would be much thinner on the ground. The world moves on, as it should, but learning the lessons of history can do much to improve our environment in terms of housing. There's a sweet spot between the familiar and the novel, where all the magic can happen. We just have to let it.

Good architecture doesn't have to be the preserve of the wealthy, corporate or civic, which it almost always is. Good architecture doesn't have to be expensive. Maybe it's time to draw the line. The population doesn't have to put up with a single toilet for a dozen people anymore, but that doesn't mean where we are is where we could be. The caricature of 'streets in the sky' highlights the less dramatic, but no less real, negative forces that can inhibit the flourishing of a neighbourhood's richness. We're paying Selfridges prices for Primark accommodation. Maybe it's time we put an end to second-rate structures and developments once and for all. Ironically, we could benefit from some of the vision, drive, inspiration and enthusiasm for housing that existed in the 1960s. As long as it's combined with a little more insight and wisdom. And maybe even a smattering of appropriately designed deck access.

blueprints for the soul

You can put down a bad book; you can avoid
listening to bad music; but you cannot miss the
ugly tower block opposite your house.

RENZO PIANO, ARCHITECT[6]

theme five

Design doesn't take
place in a vacuum.

the things
we think and
do not say

blueprints for the soul

The 1996 film *Jerry Maguire* is famous for three things even to this day. The first is, 'You had me at hello'; the second, 'Show me the money'. The third is an early scene in the film, where sports agent Jerry, played by Tom Cruise, is experiencing a growing alarm over the increasingly pernicious aspects of the way he's expected to do business. In a moment of alcohol-induced epiphany, he's inspired to write a mission statement, which he admits, having suddenly 'lost the ability to bullshit', is rather touchy-feely. He entitles it 'The Things We Think and Do Not Say'.[1]

Most of you will have a drawer or cupboard in your home where things you don't quite know what to do with are placed. Things you can't easily categorise, things you don't really want, things you might want one day. Things you believe you'll deal with at a later date or secretly don't want to deal with at all. Leftover Allen keys courtesy of Ikea, an unfortunate Christmas present from Auntie Ellie, dead batteries that just might have a bit of life in them in a crisis. You might call this drawer the shadow drawer. If the drawer or cupboard gets too full and has been neglected for too long, the mere thought of sorting it out can give you a headache. Sometimes it's easier just to forget about it or pretend it isn't really there. If a visitor to your home opened the cupboard or drawer you might feel a degree of embarrassment or even shame. One is reminded of the episode of *Friends* where the pristine, tidy, organised Monica Geller opens the cupboard we've never seen inside to reveal an overspilling mass of mess.

It's not just literal drawers or cupboards that are a shadow. We humans have all manner of metaphorical dark corners. They can be the repository of unwanted feelings, things we don't want to admit about ourselves or others, things we aren't willing to address, things we don't even know we've put in there until the drawer collapses under the weight of them. Those pounds we're going to shed starting on the tomorrow that never comes. Those resentments about certain people we can never quite bring ourselves to confront. The thoughts we have that might be unacceptable to others. It's not always bad things we send to the shadows. If we've been hurt by love, our capacity to place our heart in the hands of another can be banished to the darkness. Surrounded by cruelty and brutality, we may exile our compassion as a matter of emotional survival. The poet and author Robert Bly refers to this kind of shadow as 'The Bag', which unlike the drawer that can be closed and forgotten, at least temporarily, constantly follows in our wake.[2] We drag it around for so long we forget a time it wasn't scraping and clattering along the floor behind us. We forget that what it contains might be useless, or obsolete, or downright toxic. Or in dire need of attention and some tender, loving care. We don't notice how detrimental it's become to our lives. This principle, too, can apply to a community, a society or an industry.

In the previous chapters, we've described some of these shadows with regard to the world of everyday construction. The good things banished and the bad things denied. The perils of arrogance, the poor quality of housing developments, the Design and Build contracts, how bad buildings are affecting health and happiness. The loss of soul in our built environment that denies the need to appreciate and connect. The beauty and life that could be. They're spectres clinging to the dark side of the monolith. They lie neglected and desperate for change. But the dark shadow runs so deep, the bag is so full and we're so, so busy, the prospect of trying to tip it out, shed what's useless and damaging and bring what isn't into the light can be overwhelming. Nevertheless, the choice is simple. We can leave them in the twilight world until it's too late, or we can turn to face them and bring them into the light. Then we can nourish those things that feed the soul of architecture and eliminate those things that starve it.

The 20th century could well be termed the machine age, although it's fair to say that the machine age started well before then. The spinning jenny, a multi-spindle spinning frame that industrialised textile manufacture, was invented in the 1760s. But we can make a distinction between the machines themselves and their gradual absorption into a way of thinking, a way we touched upon in our chapter on 'streets in the sky' (see Chapter Five). As the 1900s progressed, in many aspects of life, anything that was not 'scientific' and 'rational' was increasingly banished to the shadows and often for the better. One can't underestimate the power of science and mechanisation. While, like everything else, it has its dark side, its positive impact upon our health and standard of living is incalculable. The same can't be said for our wellbeing, however. Our feelings of life satisfaction. Wellbeing requires the less tangible but nevertheless crucial aspects of life such as love, meaning, purpose, identity, connection, culture and beauty. Science and logic are important, they just aren't everything. There are levels on which the mechanistic view fails us, especially on the more ethereal and unconscious levels of human existence. We're back in baby and bathwater territory.

There's something called the rule of unintended consequences. That is, when we make a decision, enact a policy, set upon a path, there are always consequences we can't foresee. There are literally billions of examples of unintended consequences, from the small acts of individual lives to substantial acts of social engineering and all points in between.

St Peter's Precinct Shopping Centre in Oldham was built in 1967.[3] It was meant to be a flagship retail destination but its exposed, roofless layout and wind tunnel created by a subway link resulted in the population having to battle a bone-chilling gale every time they went shopping. Locals nicknamed it 'Windy City'. These conditions arose as an unintended consequence of the design.

One might think that in these days of high science and computer modelling, issues of wind would no longer be problematic, but unintended consequences can still occur.[4] A wind analysis was conducted for the 110m-tall Bridgewater Place in Leeds, completed in 2007. Nevertheless, in 2011, a man died and a woman was seriously injured after being crushed by a lorry that tipped over in strong winds next to the building. Leeds City Council later revealed that the wind tunnel effect had caused 25 'incidents'.

There are also wind issues of a different kind in these modern times.[5] The Beetham Tower in Manchester, which stands at 169m and was completed in 2006, had a rather individual problem. When strong winds moved across the fins at the top of the building, a stentorian hum was emitted, likened to an alien spaceship coming in to land. Despite the considerable modern skills, knowledge and technology that serve to analyse the likely impact of wind, unintended consequences are still with us.

Perhaps the most important lessons about unintended consequences of any kind are a) to accept that they're an omnipresent feature of human life and b) that we must be willing to recognise them, rather than deny them, and take appropriate action when required. Like consulting with acoustic experts to resolve the Beetham Tower hum, or admitting the consequences of our decisions, even if the outcome is far from what we intended.

Humankind's concentration on fast-paced rationality has created a shift in perspective where the potential of everyday architecture no longer has one foot in the world of those artistic endeavours that elevate the human spirit, such as music, painting and literature. Instead, its priority is the most basic consideration of purpose, of 'what we can get away with'. It has no care for the aspiration to transcendence. It fails to recognise the concept of something greater than ourselves that forms the heart of such things as religion, nature, community or the pursuit of excellence. And when we lose belief in that, there are unintended consequences. In terms of the built environment, one of them is a lack of humility. Humility is not self-effacing meekness or submissive weakness. It's an other-centred attitude of modesty where we place that something greater than ourselves before our own petty interests. A lack of humility is arrogant and superior, caring only for selfish desires. We see this lack of humility in many forms and many places within the world of construction; indeed, it often leads to a chain of further unintended consequences. Our 'streets in the sky' saga is the epitome of lack of humility. Fundamentally, it was a social experiment, which would have been fine if it had been kept to a single, small-scale project that was monitored over time. If that had happened, the evidence that it just didn't work would have presented itself fairly quickly and the experiment wouldn't have been repeated. Instead, the combination of fashionable philosophy, untested theories, architectural vanity and the lure of a cheap, quick fix made it a costly disaster.

A lack of humility skulks in the diminishing role of the talented, committed architect in our everyday buildings. It sniggers at the casual, pretentious pomposity of some academics and critics. It rubs its hands with glee at those whose primary concern is the pursuit of ambition to the detriment of the community, longevity or even safety. It worships at the altar of conceit. It sends all related inconveniences to the shadows. It's the mechanistic, functional, 'head' view that leads us here, this place where we don't consider the big picture, the greater good, the human soul, whatever you believe it to be. This place where the fact we despoil on a daily basis is conveniently ignored. This place where we bulldoze eternal qualities without a second thought. The soul of everyday architecture, like beauty, has become a dirty word. The ship has slipped its moorings and is drifting dangerously close to the rocks. A course correction is urgently required, hard to port.

It's easy to apportion blame, especially when the object of the blame may seem distant. And while the blame game may offer emotional satisfaction, it does nothing to resolve matters. We are where we are. We can look back to see what can be learned from the mistakes of the past and ensure they're not repeated. We can highlight where things are going wrong in the present so we can put them right. It behoves each individual and organisation to take courage and face some difficult questions about whether they're part of the problem and if they are, consider how they might become part of the solution.

'First do no harm' is a phrase every medical student quickly learns. 'First do no harm' should apply equally to the built environment. It's not a toy to be played with or a matter to be treated with casual disregard. It's imperative we stop thinking of the built environment as something that 'happens' to us. Something that's perhaps not even any of our business when in fact, it's all our business. We are all custodians of the land and everything that takes place within it. We should see the built environment as part of nature, rather than a force separated from it, and treat it with the same level of care that we now express towards the rest of the environment. The pollution of the air we breathe has long been a matter of profound concern and has generated any number of Acts of Parliament. The pollution of health, hearts and minds that a poor built environment creates should also concern us on the deepest level.

Yes, the dark shadow runs so deep, the bag is so full and we are so, so busy, the prospect of trying to tip it out, shed what's useless and damaging and bring what isn't into the light can be overwhelming. We suffer from housing difficulties and the demand for more commercial buildings: thinking, and not for the first time in our history, that faster, cheaper, easier will make all the problems go away and end in a golden sunset. Just how many cautionary tales do we need? We encounter planning practices where the left hand doesn't seem to know what the right hand is doing. We contend with procurement policies that conspire against excellence and longevity. On and on it goes. The dark shadow runs so deep, the bag is so full and we are so, so busy. Where do we start?

It is alarming that publications devoted to architecture have banished from their pages the words Beauty, Inspiration, Magic, Spellbound, Enchantment, as well as the concepts of Serenity, Silence, Intimacy and Amazement.
LUIS BARRAGÁN, ARCHITECT[6]

theme six

It's time to empty the bag and sort out the mess.

92

the architecture
of belonging

We start with those things that refuse to lie down and die. They crouch in the shadows waiting patiently, endlessly. Their innate nature can't be destroyed, it can only be hidden. They wait for the light to make them plump and sturdy again. We start with the enduring nature of place.

Place is a word that can have a lot of meanings. It doesn't just relate to where we are physically in space, place can be somewhere within ourselves; we speak of being in a good or bad place. Those places we inhabit on the outside have a profound effect on the ones we experience on the inside. But what do we mean by place and why does it matter?

We can refer to pretty much anywhere as a place in its general sense: a field, an ocean, a house. In this instance, we can refer to a place as a bounded area of more than one building that's defined by its purpose, geography, identity or our attachment to it. In this definition, a village is a place, so is an industrial estate or a housing development. Places can relate to bigger places or smaller ones, but there's always an identifiable, unifying factor within them.

Places are like people. They're formed by their geography, history, culture and the level of care and investment that's been offered to them. They can thrive on love, understanding and attention, or crumble through neglect, abuse and misunderstanding. They're generally most happy when they have a secure identity, a pleasing environment, a sense of community and a purpose. They're generally most miserable when they drift into isolation, aimlessness, confusion and degeneration. Places matter to us a great deal.

At its most primordial level, place relates to safety from predators and unpleasant surprises. When we're tucked into our home or workplace we usually feel relatively secure from threat, but once we enter the public realm, our feelings of safety decline, depending on where we find ourselves. Even though we may know rationally that the chances of anything bad happening to us are relatively low, our instincts cause disquiet. We sense there are people who might wish us harm and we have no wish to run into them. If we're on a well-lit street, populated with people and passing traffic, our feelings of disquiet may diminish. If we walk along a dark and deserted street alone, our feelings of disquiet increase. If the dark and deserted street is unfamiliar to us, the feelings of disquiet increase even more. We may experience an irresistible urge to glance back.

Many thousands of years ago, our first places of shelter arose from the need for safety from threat and protection from the elements. In a cave, we were safe on three sides, in time, with fire as further security. Eventually, we learned to build our own shelters and how to enclose and protect them. They became permanent features, which grew, organically. They grew for a purpose, often centred around water, fertile land, a chiefdom, or even such resources as the raw materials for forging. The people in these settlements built using the materials around them such as timber, straw, animal skins and stone. Skills were passed down, improved upon, evolved. Once upon a time, everyone knew how to build a decent shelter, the best available for the times they lived in. Over centuries, and with the development of more sophisticated techniques, building became a more specialised skill and builders were employed to create the structures people lived and worked in. Eventually, many of the settlements became permanent features. They became villages. Some villages became towns, some towns became cities.

The places we inhabit, pass through, visit and remember form part of the fabric of our lives. They play a powerful role in our identity and sense of wellbeing. They tell their own story about where we've come from and who we are, even where we're going. St Peter's Square in Manchester tells such a story and the more one knows about its history, the deeper and further the journey from nowhere to somewhere goes. The Romans had a fort just down the road, so it isn't a stretch to imagine centurions marching across what would become known as St Peter's Field, or indeed the Brigantes (the indigenous tribe), who weren't exactly thrilled about this state of affairs. This was the field on which the notorious 1819 Peterloo Massacre took place, when 18 people died and many hundreds were injured as cavalry charged into a crowd of thousands demonstrating for the right to vote. It was named Peterloo after Waterloo, as any such destructive action became a 'loo', just as nowadays scandals are called a 'gate' after Watergate.

Along with the early inns and hovels, a cradle of revolution manifested and burgeoned: industrial, social, technological. And it also became a spiritual place, where St Peter's Church once stood. Evidence of these events was long gone or long buried until a few years ago, when St Peter's Square enjoyed a major renovation. Now, the outline of the church is marked in paving stones and the Peterloo victims are celebrated in beautiful roses adorning the floor of the new library entrance. As for the rest of the occurrences and events in this chequered and dramatic history, we might speculate that they, too, have informed this place and weave around the branches of the trees, seep into the stone, rumble under the paving. A steady flow of evolution leading to the place we see before us today.

Figure 7.1 St Peter's Church, by James Wyatt, 1794, which once stood in St Peter's Square, Manchester: demolished in 1907.

Figure 7.2 One of the paving stones in St Peter's Square, Manchester, that mark the outline of St Peter's Church.

Opposite:

Figure 7.3 One of the roses that adorn the floor of the new Central Library entrance, in St Peter's Square, Manchester, remembering those who died in the Peterloo Massacre of 1819.

Figure 7.4 St Peter's
Square, Manchester,
as it is today.

Beyond this, the square might have personal memories for many, a cut-through to the university, the location of a first office job, the café where two people spent hours trying to find the right title for their book.

We humans love a square. Beyond the places we live and work in, squares in all their variety are known as 'the third space'. One might argue, along with the satisfying sense of enclosure a square creates, it's the older buildings that help to make it a somewhere, rather than an anywhere. The back of the Neo-Gothic Town Hall and its extension that gracefully follows the curve of the library, creating a glorious walkway between, or the 1823 city art gallery at the corner. These buildings say you're in Manchester and remind you Manchester has been here, growing and changing for many lifetimes. The more modern buildings comprising the square's opposite side tell us of another Manchester, of the fashion for global anonymity within our cities that some are happy to embrace while others look on in dismay. Taken as a whole, the formation of the square, the buildings old and new, the trees and tramways, the culture and commerce create a clear sense of identity. Spend time here, experience the architecture, delight the senses, make discoveries and connections, form attachments and it may turn out that you have come to love this place and feel like it loves you back. Which is exactly what a place should do.

We humans are drawn to places where we feel the hand of history. But it isn't just the history that attracts us, or the individual buildings. We're drawn to these places because they resonate deeply within us. We love their solidity and endurance, their placement, the way they are laid out, their human scale, patterns, windings, twists and turns that can seem so higgledy-piggledy and yet conspire together in a way that satisfies us. Their organic irregularity appears to offer

Figure 7.5 St Peter's Square, with Manchester Central Library in the left foreground and the Town Hall extension immediately behind it. The library rotunda and the Town Hall extension are both Grade II* listed.

a strange perfection. And it seems that most of us feel wounded when they're wiped away without a second thought. Far from our primordial needs, we have more sophisticated but equally compelling connections with regard to place. We aren't casual observers moving through the landscape as if we're watching a film. We merge with our surroundings. The melange of feelings and impressions places can arouse within us are impossible to unravel, but they most certainly exist. In an ancient place we might feel the bones of our ancestors lying beneath our feet, the layers of history, drama, struggle, conquest, tragedy and triumph that have led to the place we see before us today. There are a hundred ways that places can feel wrong, but there are definable ways that make places feel right. And while we can never re-create the layers of history – the steps worn from centuries of footfall, the creaking and cracking, the echo of age – our contemporary places can be every bit as beautiful and compelling as those that have gone before us, growing ever richer and deeper with time.

Places don't grow organically anymore because they can't. Even if we decide to build a new town or village, it has to be planned out beforehand. Likewise, our squares and leisure spaces, our parks and housing developments. In the modern world, everything must be known in its entirety before construction takes place.

Planning is important, of course. We can't have the population springing up random settlements on the banks of the River Dee or allow people who have no idea what they're doing to set about a housing development. But we need to combine the best instinctive elements of ancient and organic places with the modern need for rules and regulations, for contemporary materials and modern designs. Once lockdown began in the Covid-19 pandemic, place took on a new meaning for the majority of the population; losing the opportunity to live and roam freely offered a new perspective on the environments in which they found themselves. Factors that may once have been viewed as marginal took on an unprecedented importance. For many, the city apartment that once seemed so convenient began to feel like a form of solitary confinement. At the time, those involved in the housing sales and lettings industry reported something of an exodus from those apartments, bought or rented, to houses with gardens and garages that could be used as workspace. The pandemic shone a spotlight on what was truly important for meeting our physical and emotional needs. Once lockdown prevented people from employing their usual distractions, the shortcomings of their surroundings became noticeable in a way they'd never done before.

If we asked you to describe a bustling, sizeable village, chances are the vast majority of you would list exactly the same things. A central area for communal activity, shops, cafés, school, community centre, places of worship, perhaps, a square, marketplace and/or garden area all within walking distance. A range of housing in a variety of styles that reference the local vernacular in design and materials so that you always know and enjoy where you are. Housing that accommodates a variety of budgets and needs. Places where children can play. Places where small businesses or workshops can operate. A natural meeting with the greater countryside, perhaps connection to other villages, or a town. Opportunities for the village to evolve in an organic way. It's unlikely you'll visualise anything high-rise. Pretty much the opposite of the sprawling, anonymous housing estate that's a car drive away from the nearest retail park that's just like all the other retail parks. Amenity, community, housing, leisure, enterprise, connectedness.

If you ask many people who've outgrown their city pad where they'd prefer to live, they'll describe a reasonable approximation of your village, or at least a development that has some of its qualities: a sense of place, of being *somewhere*. And it's worth mentioning that with relatively minor variations, the basic village structure appears pretty much all over the world. But, of course, most of us don't get the opportunity to live in such places, especially as we generally pay a premium for the privilege.

The way most of us like to live is eternal and there's a difference between traditional and eternal. The traditional refers to a past time. The eternal refers to all time. If you want to see what happens when people think they can reinvent the wheel, take a look around our towns and cities. The creation of places that resonate, places that fill hearts and truly meet the eternal needs of we humans has been a long way down the list of priorities for a significant period of time. But there are glimmers of hope, scratched and bloody fingers of eternal truth fighting their way out of the shadows.

The *National Design Guide*, produced by the Ministry of Housing, Communities and Local Government (now the Department for Levelling Up, Housing and Communities), has guidelines for creating effective places.[1] It includes recommendations like a context that values local history and culture, an identity that creates character, public spaces that support social interactions and a mixture of uses and house types. Indeed, most boroughs in the country have a design guide that includes a commonality of principles for places that recognise and adequately encompass our innate human needs. Or put another way, places that lift the spirits rather than depress them. And yet, when you look around our streets, these principles are not always respected by the very organisations that recommend them.

Despite the overwhelming evidence of history, psychology, sociology and research, there's still plenty of opposition to these fundamental matters. Whether in universities or journals, architectural elites or bystanders, there are those who still believe we can throw away the rule book regarding at least some of these needs. They'll harangue with words like 'traditionalist' in the hope it will provoke a shiver of shame for the lack of cool buzzwords and unwillingness to attempt to reorder the human heart. In many ways, the term 'traditional' is a term of absurdity. The very act of creating a structure is traditional, but in this context, the word is used as a vehicle for anything that relates to a style that's gone before. But what isn't labelled as traditional today could be labelled as traditional tomorrow. From a certain perspective of meaning, it's all traditional in the end. The only question is whether it's a tradition worth keeping. In any case, the aim need not be either the traditional or the trendy. The aim should be for the eternal, expressed in all its glorious, infinite, exciting creativity.

Places that embody our eternal needs are required. Support for this idea is widespread, even though these needs may not be described by all in exactly the same terms. Nevertheless, many testify to their importance, in theory at least, including the authors of the *National Design Guide*. As do most boroughs in the country. And let's pay a little homage to architects like Aldo Rossi, Christopher Alexander and so many others, who understood these needs many, many years ago. Perhaps we might also include King Charles, who's well known for challenging many 20th-century trends such as isolated housing estates and remote shopping centres. In 2014, he produced his own 10 principles for architecture.[2] Repeatedly ridiculed for his views in the past, some of these views have now become widely accepted.

And let's not forget the public, who say things like, 'They don't build them like they used to', which is often interpreted as architectural ignorance. What the general public often lacks is the specialised language to articulate what they feel is missing, the same way they might lack the ability to articulate those pains running down their leg as sciatica. Just because you can't accurately identify the problem and give it a name doesn't mean it isn't hurting you. However much certain quarters would like to dismiss it, this elephant has no intention of leaving the room. It's time to ensure policy is put into practice. Let the evidence of history be our witness and our guide. These needs don't just exist, their satisfaction is crucial to the future of architecture. But we should also remember that even a straightforward tick list of demands can and often does create sterility and indifference in the wrong hands. And there are more encounters with the timeless to be had. It's time for the big reveal.

theme seven

There are things you just
don't mess with.

releasing architecture from the shadow

We begin life as a bundle of instincts. Comfort good, isolation bad. Fullness good, hunger bad. Burp good, wind bad. Upon entering the world, we don't sense ourselves as an individual being as such and make no real distinction between ourselves and our primary caregiver. As the months pass, we realise that all the sensations we have are contained within something. That something is our body, which we then realise is separate from all the things that take place outside it. It might be said that our body is the first structure we recognise. In time, there's an irresistible urge to put anything we can grasp into our mouths. We're driven towards motion: rolling, crawling, standing, walking. We begin to develop language by 'baby talking'. Unless there's an impairment that prevents it, all human children activate these instincts. But to do these things effectively, we need support and stimulation from those around us. If we don't receive it, we'll fail to develop normally, with consequences that can potentially affect us for the rest of our lives. This is the well-documented interplay of nature (the infant's instincts and drives) and nurture (the love, care, stimulation and encouragement the infant receives from those around them).

The built environment is our shared child. It's born with its own bundle of instincts, which must be nurtured in the right way or the child won't develop in an appropriate manner. When we unravel the knot of competing philosophies and egos, disentangle the centuries of fashion, sweep the dead leaves of getting away with it aside, we find the rendered truth and purity that thousands of years of building has bequeathed to us beneath the noise. We find the instincts, the eternal qualities that repeatedly demonstrate what's required of us. These eternal qualities are the foundation that must be present in order to bring buildings and places to life and set the stage for emotion and beauty. The eternal forms we're about to describe are the nature. The skill, understanding and creativity of the architect we're about to describe is the nurture. If the eternal nature is absent or flawed, the buildings and places will never enhance our lives. If the skill, understanding and creativity of the architect is deficient or obstructed, the buildings and places will never enhance our lives. It's that something greater than ourselves, essential to restoring the soul to our built environment and defining a new set of priorities.

We believe there are three timeless qualities that need to be present in our everyday buildings in order for them to satisfy the statements above, generate positive emotion and finally put an end to the dismal circumstances in which we find ourselves. These are the principles than can ensure the Vitruvian qualities of Commodity, Firmness and Delight can be met in every circumstance. These are the qualities that can make the world a better place for all of us:

Eternal

The building or development must be designed according to the archetypal principles of legibility and simplicity.

Harmonious

Each definable area of buildings must be in harmony with its environment and each of those buildings must be in harmony with its surroundings on every level.

Unmeasurable

The building or development must be designed and executed with an attitude of love and humility in order to create a soulful entity that generates positive connection, energy and emotion.

Now, we'll describe them in more detail.

eternal

Legibility

When we think of legibility, the most common theme that pops into people's heads is handwriting. Even in these days when typing has become the norm, we've probably all had the experience of trying to work out what an incomprehensible pattern of scribbles might actually say. And we've probably all felt the irritation and frustration of trying to do so; a thing that should be so simple, made so difficult. Legibility applies to all manner of things. Legibility is clarity and readability. The hallmark of good legibility is that you don't even notice it. Legibility is ease. In medieval times before the advent of the printing press, monks would sit for hours every day copying manuscripts. One can easily imagine the illegibility of some of their efforts if some bright spark hadn't come up with the idea of type, thus ensuring that all manuscripts could be read in the same way. Fast-forward a few hundred years and give a passing thought to road signs. A red triangle is a warning; a circle, an instruction; a rectangle, information. The fonts are clear and easy to read and always in the same style and colours, depending on whether you're on a road or motorway. So easy, you probably never give them a second thought. That's legibility in action.

But legibility also applies to architecture. Perhaps you've had the experience of confronting a sleek glass box of a building that possesses no hint of where the door is and spent more time than is decent trying to find it. And felt a little foolish and frustrated while doing so. No doubt there are those who think it's clever and/or aesthetically appealing, but the greatest majority of people who use buildings feel deeply uncomfortable if the entrance isn't easily apparent. Entrance is the primary means of flow to and from the building. If it isn't identifiable, things never seem quite right.

While navigation is the most important aspect of legibility, our other sensibilities also play their part. Bad acoustics can be part of a building's illegibility. Listening, or trying to make yourself heard, in a busy space that amplifies and echoes every sound within it can be profoundly tiresome and irritating, especially for more mature people whose hearing is perhaps not as clear as it once was. Likewise lighting that doesn't take the needs of those with less than perfect vision into account. Even our sense of touch and smell can affect how legible we find a building. Illegibility of any kind is one of the greatest enemies of positive emotion in architecture. It can leave us confused, unsettled, disorientated, out of sorts or even downright depressed.

Terminal One at Manchester Airport (1962), undergoing further refurbishment at the time of writing, has been a classic example of persistently unresolved and distressing illegibility. In its pre-refurbishment form, after passengers took the lift to check-in, the outside world rapidly disappeared from view. After a stressful and unpleasant zigzag through a windowless security section that eyed up everyone as potential enemies of the state, people were then forced to zigzag through a windowless shopping area. Even with the delights of Calvin Klein and Fat Face, bargain booze and Belgian chocolate, by the time they reached the other side of it, they were completely disorientated; an experience that most people found deeply unwelcome. Not exactly a great start to the long-awaited fun and sun of the Costa Blanca. Those of you who've run that particular gauntlet might think your feelings of vague threat and stress came from worries about losing your passport or whether you packed your medication. Think again. It remains to be seen whether the dismal configuration of Terminal One will be improved upon, but we live in hope. Contrast that experience with

Stansted Airport, designed by Norman Foster (1991), which draws our attention to flight and lightness. No matter where you are in the airport, the outside world is clearly visible, creating a pleasant sense of anticipation and allowing you to feel secure and calm in the orientation you instinctively crave.

And perhaps we might return to our old friends, Peter and Alison Smithson and the 'streets in the sky' (see Chapter Five). Of course, they weren't streets. Streets generally have an opposite side; you can walk across the street. Houses on a street usually have a back door and at least a tiny bit of outside space when you step out of it. Streets don't have a 20m drop to the ground. But in this case, the illegibility arises from a misleading sales pitch. If they'd been described as what they were, high-rise deck access flats and maisonettes, there would have been no confusion about the concept. However, one wonders if that particular description would have generated as much enthusiasm. As a replacement for conventional streets, they were illegible and their illegibility proved to cause a lot of misery and expense. But the Smithsons are by no means alone. It could be argued that the latter half of the 20th century has witnessed its fair share of illegibility in the pursuit of the 'ground-breaking', 'hip' and 'revolutionary'. The phrase 'fit for purpose' doesn't exist for no reason.

Within the design of buildings themselves, legibility is where we apply rational approaches to satisfy instincts and nurture feelings of ease, calm, harmony and delight. The most important factors for legibility in architecture are typologies, also known as archetypes. These typologies are another example of eternal qualities. They're few in number and relatively ancient in origin. The typology is basically the layout that's used; a simplistic diagram of how the building functions. It's the essence from which everything flows and if the layout is good, the building will be legible. If it's legible, we can travel through it with confidence and ease. The building offers us a satisfying emotional story that feels comfortable and safe. Good legibility means everything makes sense. You can't make up a new typology – well, you can, but it just won't work. Trying to force a new typology on the world is like trying to create a new kind of story. It's widely recognised there are and always have been only seven archetypal stories in the world: overcoming the monster, rags to riches, the quest, voyage and return, comedy, tragedy and rebirth.[1] Every legible story ever written can be placed in one of these categories, but they still enjoy scope for endless creativity. And within those story categories there are archetypal characters, the most common and well-loved being The Hero, which inspired the noted academic Joseph Campbell to write his famous classic *The Hero with a Thousand Faces*.[2] Archetypal forms are the reason we can understand a Greek myth in exactly the same way as its audience did thousands of years ago. And it's for the same reason a member of that ancient Greek audience would understand a *Marvel* film, although they might be a little overwhelmed by the means of its communication.

As Alexander Purves reports in 'The persistence of formal patterns', typologies are archetypal forms that dwell deep within the psyche of human beings.[3] We recognise and acknowledge them on every level of our being. Their nature is enduring, eternal. There can be many different buildings in many different styles, using all manner of materials and techniques, but if they're well designed and of a recognisable typology, there's every chance we can accept and respond positively to them.

There's little mileage in discussing typology with regard to housing, as the majority of everyday housing is built to a familiar and sensible layout. If we ask you to imagine a room in a house, chances are you'll visualise a rectangular room. It's very unlikely you'll picture a circle or a triangle. If we ask you to imagine walking through the front door of a house and tell us what you see, it will almost certainly be a hallway, a sitting room or a kitchen. If you opened the front door of a house and walked into a bedroom, you would very likely feel uncomfortable and bemused. Even though this might seem like a silly idea, it nevertheless makes the point. You have maps in your head, even though you might not know it. If you ask a child to draw a house, they will usually draw one with a pitched roof, one door and three windows, even if they don't live in a house that looks like that. But even though the familiar and sensible house layout is always among us, it can be greatly enhanced by a good architect who knows exactly how to make the most of it. And it's worth saying that legibility is as important to the outside as the inside.

Legibility doesn't just apply to single buildings; it can also apply to whole streets, squares, parks, villages – indeed anywhere the environment is constructed by human hands. In terms of building design, there are a number of primary patterns that make our instincts happy. Here are some of the ones described by Alexander Purves: Centric, The Atrium, The Cloister, Castle, Square and Temenos, The Linear Space, The Circulation Spine, Serial Progression, The Grid.[4]

You'll be relieved to know we're not going to explain them in all their glorious technical detail, but any architect should have more than a passing understanding of them and will know which to use according to the project, usually Centric (think of the Pantheon in Rome), which is concerned with interior volume, or Linear (the Uffizi Gallery in Florence), which is concerned with line and the experience of path.

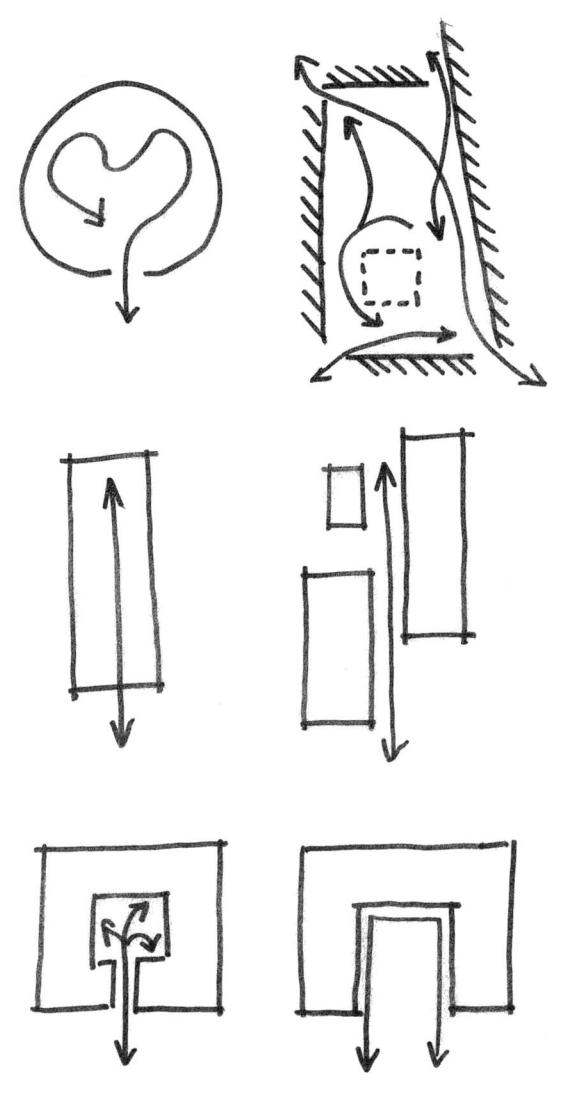

Figure 9.1 A selection of
eternal building typologies.
Left to right, top to bottom:
1 Centric; 2 Castle/Square/
Temenos; 3 Linear Space;
4 Circulation Spine; 5 Atrium;
6 Cloister.

When it comes to other kinds of everyday buildings, such as schools and workplaces, the question of typology becomes of crucial importance. Everyone has probably had the experience of walking into an unfamiliar building and wondering where on earth they're supposed to go. If that doesn't become apparent in a very short space of time, chances are you're dealing with faulty typology. That's also true if you find any aspect of your journey through it or experience of being in it unpleasant or confusing. However, there are rare circumstances where illegibility can be employed for a higher purpose, most notably in the Imperial War Museum North in Manchester, designed by Daniel Libeskind (2002).

Libeskind wanted visitors to feel the unsettling nature of war and used a variety of techniques to achieve this. The route into the museum is confusing, with the curves of the shattered globe, called 'shards', that make up the outline of the building continuing inside, which affects how people move around it. The Air Shard entrance is small, unlike the traditional grand entrance to major museums, and visitors have to follow a pattern that goes back on itself, which creates a sense of disorientation. To increase this feeling, the Air Shard is neither an indoor nor an outdoor space, which makes it both sheltered and exposed. The concrete tower in the Air Shard looks like it's leaning back when it's actually straight. There is a lack

Figure 9.2 The Imperial War Museum North, Manchester, by Daniel Libeskind, 2002. A noble exercise in deliberate awkwardness and illegibility.

of right angles in the main space and no natural light. Even the temperature fluctuates, while the floor slopes down by about 2.5m. Although we'd all struggle to tolerate these features in our everyday buildings, in this context it's a powerful and appropriate sensory experience. And the 'wrongness' of it helps us understand how important 'rightness' is. If the typology isn't right, the building will never be user friendly.

Simplicity

Beautiful simplicity is order and harmony. It's when you look at a building and are soothed by and instantly connected to what you see before you. It's when you're inside a building and everything feels as smooth as silk. It has its own elegance. You'd be forgiven for thinking it's easy, but beautiful simplicity is a most difficult thing to achieve.

That doesn't mean there isn't room for complexity in architecture, which can be wonderful and inspiring in the right proportion and in the right context, such as the Sagrada Família in Barcelona, or appropriately disruptive and disturbing, as in the case of the Imperial War Museum North. But too many shouty buildings among us are vexatious to our health and wellbeing. Our everyday buildings should promote a melodious melange of positive emotions in us and enhance the standout structures where they occur, rather than create a competing discordance that, however unconsciously, always leaves us out of sorts.

Those of you of sufficient age will remember the early days of personal computers when one was compelled to negotiate a language alien to the average user. Over time, rather than forcing us to adapt to the computer, the computer has been adapted to us. It asks you things like, 'Are you sure you want to do this?' rather than threatening you with an incomprehensible code just before the tech police burst into the room and arrest you for digital stupidity. Its language has been humanised and simplified to make sense to the average person, just as the operation of the objects themselves has been. The workings of today's computers and mobile phones are infinitely more complex than their early predecessors, but as far as the user is concerned, their complexity has been rendered into the slim elegance of comprehensibility.

Beautiful simplicity in architecture is also a distillation of the complex, an essence that can unpack itself into harmony within us. It's a composition that looks effortless and lyrical; it possesses a beautiful, rhythmic elegance that makes you feel like everything's going to be okay. It's the seafood tortellini in a lobster bisque. Unlike the plate loaded with a cornucopia of differing tastes, textures and techniques, there's really nowhere to hide. The cloak of virtue-signalling, low-carbon credentials to disguise the shortcomings will not cover the tracks. Trying to do something clever just for the sake of it won't fool anyone. Promoting it as 'cool' or 'revolutionary' can't camouflage the truth. This is a lily that can't be gilded. It doesn't distract with tricks or fads; the architectural equivalent of using a sprig of parsley to hide the blunders won't get you anywhere.

Following pages:

Figure 9.3 Holmes Road Studios, London, by Peter Barber Architects, 2019. A striking statement of beautiful simplicity.

Figure 9.4 Foundry,
Salford, by Nick Moss
Architects, 2018. An
inspiring example of just
how beautiful simplicity
can be.

A building of beautiful simplicity is true to its own inner nature. It's at peace with itself and in being so, can help us be more at peace with ourselves. And in a world that grows increasingly more complex, we often crave the restful haven of peace and simplicity wherever and whenever it's available to us.

In this context, simple does not mean 'plain', or 'boring', or 'minimal'. Holmes Road Studios in Kentish Town, London, designed by Peter Barber Architects (2019), has beautiful simplicity, as does Foundry in Salford, by Nick Moss Architects (2018). On a grander scale, the Grade I listed Piece Hall in Halifax, West Yorkshire, has it, too.

The Piece Hall, built in the late 1700s, was originally created as a collection and distribution point for trade in woollen products made in the area. With over 300 rooms that opened onto colonnaded walkways surrounding a substantial open courtyard, the Piece Hall's simple and well-functioning beauty has proved to be a prime example of useful longevity. As well as being a visitor destination purely for the architecture, thanks to a major restoration finished in 2017, it now houses artisanal shops, cafés, bars and restaurants, while its central square plays host to many social and cultural activities throughout the year. Pretty good for a development fast approaching its 250th birthday. Sadly, the name of the architect who designed it has been lost in the mists of time.

In those buildings that embody beautiful simplicity, such as the Piece Hall and Holmes Road Studios, you'll notice three fundamental qualities: satisfying proportions, a pattern of repetition and a constrained number of materials.

Many of our modern everyday buildings are relatively simple in the broadest sense of the word, but by no means beautifully so. Indeed, all too often they're quite the opposite. It's entirely possible

127

Figure 9.5 Piece Hall, Halifax, architect unknown, 1779. An enduring advertisement for the elegance of repetition and simplicity.

to see two new developments that are literally next door to each other and yet one can be ugly, awkward and dysfunctional in its simplicity and one can be beautiful. The reason for the difference is beautifully simple. It's the talent of the architect and them being allowed to do their job properly, as we described in Chapter Three. Beautiful simplicity requires the highest skill set, the deepest level of understanding and the relentless pursuit of excellence. It offers a directness of expression and an absence of pretentiousness, just like the seafood tortellini. Beautiful simplicity is created when the architect has the ability to reach the essence of something and understand what it truly is.

This essence then becomes a pure concept, which in turn permeates through every aspect of the design, where the unessential is discarded, and all the components work seamlessly together. Whether you're outside the building or inside, there's a consistent experience of clarity and wholeness. Our instincts are comforted and eased, and our aesthetic senses pleased as we experience the underlying sense of harmony that's so fundamental to our health and wellbeing.

harmonious

The crucial nature of context

Context is one of the ways we humans make sense of the world and there are few aspects of life where context is unimportant to us. We can think of context as the background that fits around the object. The object, we can think of as the thing that fits into that background. If the object is in harmony with its context, we don't miss a beat. When it's out of context, we can experience a range of emotions, from humour and surprise to confusion, displeasure or even fear, depending on the situation.

If you opened the door to your supermarket delivery driver and found them dressed as a 2m-tall rabbit, you'd certainly be surprised, and possibly shocked. However, that shock and surprise would probably turn to laughter once you'd regained your composure, as something being out of context can be an effective ingredient for humour. If you attended an Easter Fair and found yourself in the company of someone dressed as a large rabbit, it would be considerably less of a shock because it would be in context. And while the occasional out-of-context shock or surprise can be enjoyable and energising, too many of them can leave us feeling confused, chaotic and disorientated.

Within architecture, context can be seen as the web of wider interrelated conditions in which the building or buildings will occur. Buildings don't exist in isolation: even a development on a rural greenfield site has a landscape that can be negotiated and referenced. However, over much of the past century, there's been a fundamental dichotomy within architecture. Those who believe in the importance of context seek to react to surroundings and make the building work in harmony with them. The contrary view seeks to impose the building on its surroundings, regardless of what those surroundings are. That takes us back to our well-worn reference

Figure 10.1 The three stages of Hulme Crescents, Manchester.
Stage 1: Established, conventional, contextual housing in a familiar street pattern before demolition.
Stage 2: New housing is taken out of context, becoming an object in space configuration.
Stage 3: Housing is taken out of the object in space configuration and returned to a contextual design and street pattern after consultation with local residents. The 1972 housing development (Stage 2) did not consider context. This created a disturbing sense of dislocation for its residents (see Chapter Five).

point, 'streets in the sky' (see Chapter Five). Those sprawling deck access projects of the 1960s didn't just fail to take the cultural and social context into account, they also failed to take their surroundings into account. Well, they didn't fail, exactly, they just didn't think it mattered. One of the primary criticisms of Modernism is that it values the imposition of its own characteristics above all else. There are movements within architecture that don't believe context matters at all. We might call them the object-in-space brigade, but we believe that sensitivity to context firmly belongs in our great hall of eternal qualities.

The idea of imposition is perhaps far more sinister and insidious than it might seem in the first instance. It's the architectural equivalent of people telling us how to live our lives, that they're superior and can decide what's best for us. It's fundamentally totalitarian. We might be willing to tolerate a little advice on how to lead a healthy life, but at the end of the day, we can make our own choices about the bacon butty versus the smashed avocado. And most of us generally don't have a problem living within the laws created over time in a democratic society: we accept it as a common good, just as we accept the result of an election, even if it's not our preferred party. But in terms of the built environment, people who place their cult philosophies, their own importance, whims and egotistical desires above the bedrock of thousands of years of knowledge, wisdom, culture, nature, community and instinct, let alone the wishes of the population, aren't really doing us any favours. The jangling, discordant result of an architect's certainty that the built environment is a toy for them to play with is something that affects us all and in terms of everyday buildings is a recipe for displeasure. It's likely that everyone has noticed buildings that are grating, irksome, exasperating even. Their out-of-place countenance provokes uncomfortable sensations of disharmony and dislocation.

Harmonising old and new

You may recall the description of St Peter's Square, Manchester, in Chapter Seven – most specifically, a beautiful crescent-shaped walkway between two Grade II* listed buildings, the library rotunda and the Town Hall extension. Known as Library Walk, it's probably the most loved space in the whole city, where the two forms stand perfectly hand in hand, neither dominating the other. Library Walk is a shining example of context. However, in 2015, an addition to the walkway divided opinion.

The new entrance is a curved glass structure designed to connect the library and Town Hall extension together and which contains an entrance to each of them. There are further doors to allow passage through each side of Library Walk. Designed by SimpsonHaugh and Partners, the *RIBA Journal* described the award-winning project as 'a three-dimensional abstract playfulness that is at once architecture and sculpture'.[1] The new entrance is of high quality with interesting details: something that could be described as pure in form and execution. But critics of the project believe it jars with the cordial crescent created between the Town Hall extension and the library and confuses people with its entrance sign, which stands just a few metres away from the original classic portico of the library. While many believe the new entrance is an appealing solution, for those who are unhappy with it, the sense of context they loved has been lost.

Harmonising old and new is a delicate process. The International Rugby Experience by Níall McLaughlin Architects, opened in 2023, is located on the High Street in Limerick's Georgian Quarter. Thorough and sensitive research into historic civic buildings in Georgian streetscapes with reference to the scale of churches and civic halls has enabled this project to sit beautifully within its

environment. It's contextual at the lower level, stepping back in where the higher element rises above the urban block, which helps to mark the corner where it stands. Rising above the Georgian townhouse terraces creates a similarity to the Augustine Church just down the road, but it still ties with the height of the building opposite. The museum is substantial and dignified; a brick tower fused to a lower block, matching the parapet height of the Georgian buildings that surround it. A large area of high-level glazing helps to reduce the tower's bulk; there are many ways in which this building understands it doesn't need to shout. The solidity of the material grounds it within its historic streets. Its red brick feels contextual, but the immediately dominant material is a paler render. This museum pays homage to Georgian-era traditions without becoming a copy. It's a building of its time and of all time.

In our daily lives, we often find our relationship to and understanding of other people is greatly enhanced when we can put them in context. When we take the trouble to know their background, likes and dislikes, strengths and weaknesses, circumstances and challenges they face, we're much better equipped to connect with them. When we know a person's story, we develop a contextual mental picture of who they are and can proceed in our relationship with them on that basis. From knowing exactly which birthday present to buy them to recognising the signs they're secretly distressed, context helps us to optimise our relationships with others.

Figure 10.2 Library Walk, Manchester. Glorious context and harmony weave their magic between the two buildings, while the new entrance divides opinion.

137

A similar process operates regarding context in architectural design, but of course the 'person' (the building) doesn't yet exist. It's the context that helps to give form to the 'person'. It's part of a multifaceted process by which the site tells the architect what it wants to be. Clearly, in the case of the International Rugby Experience in Limerick, someone was listening.

Working to context is a kind of accountability to and respect for surroundings, which can include the historical, physical and cultural. A deep understanding of everything that encompasses a site encourages a responsive approach. It's probably easier to say what context isn't rather than what it is because it's a different thing every time. It's definitely not mock Tudor, a kind of 'style mashing' with whimsical references to the past that often lack material honesty. Neither does it mean that if the development is going to be on a street of red-brick buildings, it has to be in red brick. (Planning departments, please take note. No, really, please.) In fact, slavish copying of any kind is really not what context is about. It's far more subtle and intricate than that. And it should be said that place as described at some length in Chapter Seven is also context. For a skilled architect, that rich tapestry of qualities can generate works that are original and beautiful, but never out of keeping. With enough awareness and sensitivity, the architect can create a vision that resonates with everyone who belongs to the locale, that encapsulates and accommodates all the seen and unseen forces that are brought to bear upon it.

Figure 10.3 The International Rugby Experience, Limerick, by Niall McLaughlin Architects, 2023. A deceptively skilful blending of old and new illustrates a great example of context.

Figure 10.4 The Hallé extension in Cutting Room Square, Manchester, by Stephenson Hamilton Risley Studio, 2019, enjoys an agreeable harmony with its surroundings. The building sits in the heart of Manchester's Ancoats, once an old and decayed industrial area reborn into a thriving locale with apartments, businesses, shops, cafés and restaurants.

unmeasurable

Love

We interact with the buildings around us with our whole being, whether we're consciously aware of it or not. When we dream, we often experience environments barely registered or known in our waking lives, only to find they appear in meticulous detail. Such is the power of the unconscious. In a building that doesn't please the instincts and sensibilities, these unconscious forces can induce a range of negative emotions, such as anxiety, dread or irritability. The reason for this is that our 'self' merges with the building's 'self', and this merging involves all of our senses and associations. Just as another person can make us feel uncomfortable, so can a building. A procession of buildings that cause discomfort is like a procession of people who cause discomfort and, ultimately, it will take its toll.

All the time we're experiencing a building our brain is calculating in the background. Is it threatening or benign? Is it beautiful or ugly? Do I want to be inside this place or get the hell out? What do I see, smell, touch, hear? Every building we encounter acts as an extension of ourselves and stimulates a range of emotions, sensations and impressions within us. With each building we encounter, we become a slightly different person. Religious buildings seek to turn our attention heavenwards and celebrate the glory of God. The Imperial War Museum North (see Chapter Nine) offers us a hint of the jarring, splintering dislocation of conflict. Great palaces have been designed to impress and intimidate. If buildings weren't capable of having a profound effect on us, we wouldn't bother to make one any different from another. But what of our everyday buildings, the structures where the greatest part of human life takes place? Is a house or apartment merely a place where we're stored between visits to the outside world? Is the office merely a place where we're machines of production? Indeed, they are not. They're worlds in themselves and you might ask yourself, in this respect, what kind of world you deserve. Should you have to tolerate the lifeless, ugly, hollow and impersonal? Are these the words you would want to punctuate your life? There are other words, words that aren't really talked about anymore, words that hang silent and heavy in the air. Words like beauty, connectedness, love, care and empathy.

Even if we evolve matters to meet the needs of those immutable instinctive blueprints, if we incorporate the placemaking, legibility, simplicity and context, we must infuse these elements with something else. Our shared child, the built environment needs more than the satisfaction of those fundamental drives. Our child needs love. While those eternal qualities we've already described are part of love, perhaps even the foundations for it, we must attend to the more ethereal worlds and emotional words that are taking such a beating in our everyday buildings.

The fact is, for all the struggles and headaches, most architects love what they do. However, this doesn't always mean they're capable of infusing that love into their designs. That's generally a force that flows beneath a thousand technical and practical design considerations that not everyone can access. It's an unconscious force that can't be taught, but can be encouraged. The only way you can know if an architect designs lovingly is by looking at their work because when they do, it's there for all the world to see … and feel.

Love may seem a strange word to use in the somewhat rugged world of construction but perhaps we can unpeel it into the familiar. We talk of an item being 'lovingly restored', artisans often use the phrase 'lovingly created' or 'lovingly designed'. We speak of people 'putting their heart into it'. What do we mean by designing with love? When we use or encounter these terms, what exactly is being

143

conveyed? The impression we often have in these circumstances is that the creator or designer has gone the extra distance and put something of themselves into the work they've done. That they've called upon everything within themselves to create something unique and beautiful. And that unique thing will infuse its love into you, lift your heart and satisfy your need for that beauty. Sadly, lovingly designed isn't always well designed. Love without skill leads to lack, as does skill without love.

It can become difficult for architects to access that love. In any profession that requires intense training, long hours and great responsibility, like law, medicine or architecture, as far as the workplace is concerned, emotion is of necessity quashed under the weight of other considerations. But there's no requirement for doctors and lawyers to traverse the path between the aesthetics and emotionality of art and the rationality of science. On the one hand, construction is a tough business and when it comes to the nuts and bolts, emotional and artistic considerations should be put firmly in their place. If everyone concerned doesn't do their job properly, buildings can leak or weather badly, chunks of them can fall away, stairs can collapse, cracks can appear and, in the worst-case scenario, people can die. Let's face it, we'd no more want a site manager sobbing over a difficult construction issue than we'd want a paramedic sobbing over the injured victim of a car accident. But that's only one side of the coin. It's the dedicated architect alone who walks between worlds, who commits to blend the mass of technical considerations into a seamless relationship with the quest for beauty.

Over the course of years, further pressures can contribute to the suppression of emotion for the architect, not least of which are the brutal circumstances in which they can be placed in terms of getting business and in trying to maintain the integrity of a project, such as the procurement process we described in Chapter Three. This is further compounded by the fact the average practice owner needs an ego the size of a house to even survive the slings and arrows of the industry. For some, putting ego to one side and accessing the insights can become a labyrinth that can't be negotiated. Given those pressures and circumstances, it's perhaps remarkable how many architects can still plumb the depths, access those mysterious, hidden corners of the psyche and breathe love into every aspect of their designs. Given the opportunity, however humble the building, their work glows with enchantment and life.

Most architects would probably rather die than even consider using these emotional words with regard to a project. They'd certainly cringe. One can easily imagine the hysterical laughter that would ensue if an architect walked into a developer's office and stated they'd like to design a housing development with love and tenderness in mind. A development that offered sanctuary, harmony and beauty, that inspired the best within us. Worse still if they said the whole process should be conducted with humility. But actually, there's a perfectly rational and commercial basis for designing with love. We don't have to call it love: we could call it care, empathy, passion or commitment, or all of the above, but love will do. Without exception, good architecture is always a labour of love. This isn't floppy, soppy love, this isn't a bleeding heart in brick form. It's tough love, gritty love, it's passion for architecture, for the project. It's a love that will go the extra distance to protect the integrity of the project

Following pages:

Figure 11.1 Maggie's Centre, Manchester, by Foster + Partners, 2016. A little love goes a long way.

and dig deep for the best solution. We sometimes refer to this kind of love as vocation or dedication. More aligned with obsession than pleasure, this love shouldn't suggest a state of happiness. You could describe it as an attitude.

Just as when we feel love for a person, love for an activity is a highly motivating factor in the pursuit of excellence. It makes us try harder, reach deeper, aim higher. It sustains us when the odds are against us or we feel like giving in. Love creates empathy; for the design, its environment and for the people who'll ultimately encounter it. Love opens the door to those deep creative places where all the magic lies. Without love, there can never be true architectural competence. From the beauty of the designs, to the quality of the materials and construction, in commercial terms, working with love ultimately offers more bang for your buck.

Although they aren't everyday buildings and certainly aren't cheap, the Maggie's Centres for cancer sufferers are a fine example of designing with love. At the time of writing, there are 22 Maggie's Centres in the UK, generally designed by high-profile architects such as Frank Gehry, Richard Rogers, Zaha Hadid and Norman Foster. The Maggie's Centres emphasise the qualities of Maggie Keswick Jencks's original vision: an open 'kitchen' area, well-lit, spacious sitting rooms, access to a garden or greenery and, wherever possible, stunning natural vistas. Maggie's Centres aspire to be a warm, welcoming sanctuary that creates the best possible emotional impact on its users and, generally speaking, they're quite beautiful. But what's perhaps most striking is the attitude of tenderness that's so clearly demonstrated in every part of the architecture, from the design and materials used to the furnishings inside them. No one tries to be clever for the sake of it in a Maggie's, no one tries to cheapen it as a matter of routine. No one says,

'That'll do.' No one dismisses the fundamental needs of its users because those needs are recognised as absolute. The creation of a Maggie's is the embodiment of designing with love and humility. There's no earthly reason why at least a little of that love and humility can't be incorporated into our experience of the wider built environment. While we may not all have to endure the devastating effects of cancer, there'll be many points in our lives when we, too, will need beauty, sanctuary and comfort to help us deal with inevitable onslaughts and tragedies.

Conversely, a lack of love leads to indifference and merely paying lip service to the activity. It leads to a selfish, short-term state of mind and making the minimum contribution necessary. A lack of love is the epitome of 'what we can get away with'. The fact is, if it hasn't been designed with love and consequently constructed with reasonable fidelity to that love, the chances are it won't be architecture. Many of you will recall the Marble Arch Mound debacle in London in 2021, where what should have been a pleasing design and interesting perspective on the Marble Arch monument and surrounding area basically turned into a heap of mud. In an unusual move for a firm of architects, MVRDV, who were the original designers of the project and who were most displeased with an end result that was not of their making, expressed their feelings publicly. The term they used is interesting. They called what happened a 'loveless execution'.[1] In this situation, it's worth using the word 'execution' in both of its meanings.

The love of which we speak has no time for cultish philosophies or fashionable design agendas. Its primary ambition isn't to impress, get peer approval or win awards (which isn't to say that the awards aren't more than welcome if they do happen to turn up). Its focus is to design the best possible building for the people who see and use it.

We greet the buildings around us with our instincts and senses. We interact with them with our whole being, whether we're consciously aware of it or not. The question is, how do you want your everyday buildings to greet you? With warmth and pleasure or hostility and disregard? There are times when lack of love lies in the original design and times when it lies in the execution. From the dispiriting housing developments to the ugly, ill-considered commercial buildings, we're stuck with them for a long time. For those of you familiar with epic family car journeys, the next time you try a game to relieve the boredom, instead of playing I Spy, try playing 'spot the everyday building designed and constructed with love'. You may find they're a dying breed. The time to enact a zero-tolerance policy on indifference is long overdue. It would be helpful to put those architects who have the ability and will to design with love in a better position because love leads to soul and, ultimately, it's the soul that creates the energy and emotion we're so starved of in our everyday buildings.

Soul

Soul can be a tricky word. It has many connotations. But when we say a thing has soul, for most people, there's an intuitive consensus about the meaning. We recognise it whenever it manifests, whether that be through a painting, a piece of music, a novel or architecture. Or even through a meaningful encounter with another human being. Soul is a sense of engagement that resonates within us,

Figures 11.2a and 11.2b
The Marble Arch Mound, London, by MVRDV, 2021. A pleasing design that was ultimately the victim of a 'loveless execution' created by value engineering.

a positive emotional union with an external object. And there's something about it that's profoundly sustaining. Good soul is a beautiful thing. Within architecture, the soul of a building is the sum greater than its parts. This is the fairy-dust department, where science is but a speck in the distance. This is the thing we all recognise and yet can never fully describe.

But there are rules that come before soul. In order for us to engage with it, there has to be a recognisable medium of communication. For instance, each musical symphony that's written is created through a complex set of rules – musical scales, timing, movements, orchestra parts and so forth – which must be brought together into a coherent whole. The idea is already present before these rules are set in motion, the story and the emotion that will captivate us are merely waiting for the structure that will communicate it effectively. But if the structure is wanting, it doesn't matter how beautiful the original intentions are because we'll never experience them.

A building with soul can kindle an uplifting experience within us. Many buildings with soul can create an incalculable enhancement to our lives. Like the attitude of love, soul can't be taught, although with sufficient will and courage to look within, there is potential to find it. Without it there can be competence, but not transcendence.

It's said that the good architect doesn't hit their full stride of potential until well into their 40s. That's how long it takes to be able to synthesise all the qualities we've described to you during the course of our journey. We generally call this facility intuition, but that need not be an elusive term. Intuition comprises advanced technical skill, experience and a rich store of information about all the architecture that's been seen and studied. It's deep knowledge and understanding of context, of materials, of human need and of beauty. It's the innate sense of eternal themes. It's a lifetime of striving, but rather than these qualities being individual components of the art, they are so familiar, so understood, so second nature that they appear as a whole concept from the very beginning, right through to the very end. And if there's anybody out there who thinks someone other than the trained architect can achieve this magnificent and spectacular feat of synthesis and soul, do let us know.

Without the unmeasurable, there'll be no delight, no emotion, no beauty. The unmeasurable is exactly what so many of our modern everyday buildings don't have, owing to a lack of recognition that it matters or the inability to acknowledge it even exists. The combination of qualities we've described is capable of producing engaging, interesting, unique and state-of-the-art architecture that we can all enjoy and appreciate for many years to come. And once these qualities are woven gracefully together like a murmuration of starlings, in their fruition they become a beautiful whole. When that happens, the unmeasurable manifests in all its inspirational glory. The divine spirit of Foundry (see Chapter Nine); the warm, enveloping arms of Holmes Road Studios (see Chapter Nine); the timeless eloquence of Magdalene College Library, Cambridge, designed by Níall McLaughlin Architects. We experience them here and there, the pure, everyday architectural moments that have been allowed to flourish and enrich us like an occasional orchid among the hogweed. And if they exist, they're possible. And if they're possible, we can make them probable. Why settle for anything less?

A great building, in my opinion, must begin with the unmeasurable, must go through measurable means when it is being designed, and in the end must be unmeasurable.
LOUIS KAHN, ARCHITECT[2]

Figure 11.3 Magdalene
College Library, Cambridge, by
Níall McLaughlin Architects,
2021. An inspiring example of
beautiful, thoughtful design
in complete harmony with
its surroundings, evoking a
wonderful sense of emotional
completion and soulful
appreciation.

Figure 11.4 Once the eternal qualities are woven gracefully together like a murmuration of starlings, in their fruition they become a beautiful whole.

theme eight

The truth is out there. Eternal.
Harmonious. Unmeasurable.

a line in the sand

There's a relationship you've had since the day you were born and you'll have it until the day you die. But there's a problem in this relationship: you might say it's become dysfunctional. The relationship is between you and the state of the buildings that surround you.

Architecture is the ultimate expression of human civilisation. From Stonehenge to Liverpool Anglican Cathedral, it's where everything we've been, that which we are and may become is expressed and held firm for us. We would know little, if anything, of many ancient worlds without the discovery of their buildings, occasionally intact, often skeletal, but nevertheless containing details of the lives that people led and the times they lived in.

Architecture offers us something to hold fast to in an unstable world. It wraps our history around us, it expresses our values, it literally gives structure to our society. When we see scenes of modern warfare, along with the horror and distress we feel for the people who are casualties of it, we grieve for the bombed-out buildings, the shattered, hollow husks of what used to offer stability, security and a sense of permanence to those lives. Our hearts sink when, among the rubble, we see a child's shoe, a brown and blistered photograph or the shattered evidence of a table where a family once chatted as they ate. We see how easily chaos can come knocking at the door. And when the war is over, once the population is fed, medical needs attended to, temporary schools adapted, makeshift shelter erected, the first thing we do is rebuild. And if we're wise, we rebuild with the eternal patterns, grids, qualities and memories of that which has gone before as our guide. Thus begins renewal and continuity. In rebuilding, we attend to our collective soul. In expressing those qualities in new and beautiful ways, we create faith in the future. It's often said that the attitude of a country is described by how it treats its prisoners. Perhaps it's also described by how we treat our buildings. In the UK, it seems that we've frequently replaced one kind of scar with another. We haven't done our shared child justice. Our surroundings aren't what they could be. And consequently, neither are we.

We've taken you on a journey through the eternal qualities we believe to be self-evident; eternal qualities that must be accepted if places and buildings are to have any hope of possessing the soul that can transmit positive emotion. Getting to a point where that can happen can feel so impossibly complex and unobtainable that it's easier to leave it in the shadows and turn away, accept the status quo and pretend the wound doesn't exist. But in reality, it's actually quite simple. The seismic shift doesn't have to leave chaos in its wake. This seismic shift requires only a change of perspective. As earthquakes go, it barely need register on the Richter scale. The eternal qualities we've described are our baseline, the fundamental principles from which everything must flow. We take these truths from the bottom of the priority pile and place them at the top. They direct the policies and practices, rather than the other way round. There's nothing unrealistic in the request for everyone involved in the construction industry to adopt them. Certainly, there are barriers to be negotiated, which we have touched upon and will reaffirm. But these barriers can be removed once the need to shift priorities is accepted.

The first is the training the architect undergoes. The traditional culture of architectural education doesn't always impart the appropriate messages to the student. High marks are often awarded to the shouty, self-important, overly complex designs that bear little relation to context, however absurd or impractical they might be. This can indoctrinate students into thinking they have to be constantly 'clever' and 'different' in the most unsubtle of ways.

Everyone knows the story of 'The Emperor's New Clothes'. While as an occasional exercise, this kind of project can be useful, inspiring and educational, it should by no means be the primary mode of teaching. The fact is, once qualified, over 90% of architects will never design a building of this kind, which may leave them unprepared for what they could be capable of offering to the everyday built environment, instead of the inconsistent mess that we often currently experience.

Although they're often qualified architects, many academics have little experience of being in practice, therefore, it would be helpful to access more experienced architects alongside them to teach and guide students. This mindset that begins at university often carries over into the workplace, which can give priority to values that not only ignore, but actively dismiss, the importance of eternal qualities, leading to showy, inappropriate, short-term designing, which ultimately lets us all down.

The construction industry, too, would benefit from a shift in priorities. The process of procurement has been described in some detail (see Chapter Three), demonstrating what a devastating effect it can have on the quality of our shared child, the built environment. Each and every one of us has the right to demand a decent standard of architecture and the role of the architect in the fulfilment of that quest needs to be reconsidered. These buildings are being constructed anyway, and a beautiful, well-functioning building doesn't have to cost any more or take any longer to construct than an ugly, impractical one. The major housebuilders, too, might consider a greater role for architects in their developments because there's a legitimate question as to whether anyone else can effectively take a project from the unmeasurable, through the measurable and back to the unmeasurable, as we've described in Chapter Eleven.

However imperfectly they may operate in reality, there are areas of life where we have clear expectations. We expect our medical staff to put the wellbeing of the patient above all else; we expect our lawyers to do the utmost for their clients; we expect our teachers to make the education of our children their first priority. That doesn't mean the joys of commerce and profit can't enter into such equations where and when appropriate, it simply means those pursuits should take place within a set of boundaries as to what is and isn't acceptable. It's time to put architecture deeper into the arena of expectation than it already is. An expectation based on the three principles (Eternal, Harmonious, Unmeasurable) that makes quality and beauty a given. And there are compelling reasons why.

We spend most of our time in and around buildings and those buildings can have a profound effect on our physical, emotional and spiritual wellbeing. There can be little doubt that an improvement in architecture would create a significant enhancement in people's lives. While a large-scale study on the above is currently unavailable, there has been significant application of scientific method with regard to specific areas. One much-cited classic example is the 1984 study by Roger S. Ulrich, 'View through a window may influence recovery from surgery'.[1]

Ulrich examined records of patients in a Pennsylvania hospital between 1972 and 1981. He wanted to determine whether a hospital room with a window and view of a natural setting might influence patient recovery. He discovered that 23 surgical patients assigned to rooms with windows looking out onto a natural scene had shorter post-operative hospital stays than those who didn't. There were also fewer negative evaluative comments in nurses' notes and the patients needed fewer painkillers than 23 patients in similar rooms that had windows opposite a brick wall.

There are interesting experiments, too. In *Alchemy*, Rory Sutherland suggests the possibility that putting shutters on shops increases the incidence of crime, as it suggests the area is already lawless.[2] He describes an experiment created by Tara Austin, who'd encountered research that suggested images of cute, wide-eyed young children's faces have a calming effect on people. Faces such as these were then painted on shop shutters. Sutherland concludes it appeared to significantly reduce crime and did so for very little financial investment, as opposed to the considerable expense of extra police or more CCTV.

Studies and experiments such as this abound: reactions to daylight, ventilation, access to nature, colour, blank streetscapes, busy streetscapes, even such topics as ceiling height and performance. The list is long and getting longer. All these hundreds, if not thousands, of studies endlessly highlight the observation that even subtle attributes within the built environment can have a profound impact on us. And while these scientific studies relate to worthwhile things, they're by no means everything.

The lack of emotion and beauty in our built environment isn't a dramatic, full-frontal attack on us, it's a steady drip, drip, drip that ultimately wears away at even the most hardy human. It has more in common with vitamin deficiency than the flu.[3] But we should nevertheless remember that both those particular maladies can result in profound ill health, lasting side effects and even death. We often bemoan the antisocial activities that take place in run-down, neglected areas and generally assume it's the behaviour that leads to the area being run-down, when it may well be that the area itself is making a major contribution to wearing the people within it down. We might say that such places are suffering from a lack of iron and vitamin C. Tara Austin's experiment with children's faces contains a powerful hint in that direction.

In a good built environment that feels alive and engaged, that feels like it cares, we ourselves can be more alive and engaged. Just as our interactions with people can influence our mood, our interactions with the built environment act in much the same way. Each ugliness of countenance, each difficulty of navigation, each lack of harmony, each advertisement of neglectful thinking creates stress within us. In the worst-case scenario, in the worst examples of cheap indifference and hollow dysfunctionality, it can lead us into despair. Most of us find the modern world stressful enough, without having to spend our lives in environments that stress us more. What we actually need are environments that stress us less. Stress is cumulative and can come from a multitude of sources: money worries, difficulties at work, discontent with our relationships. But the stress all pours into a single pool and our built environment is conspiring to fill that pool to the point where it overflows.

But this isn't just about mitigating negative states, it's about encouraging positive ones. When the built environment degrades, the quality of both personal and collective civic life degrades with it. Good architecture nurtures. It encourages, rather than diminishes. It's like a friend who understands you. It creates the circumstances where we can satisfy our instincts, feel safe and connected and absorb the positive emotional energy in our surroundings that can only enhance our being.

The last, and equally compelling, reason for an improvement in everyday architecture is one of legacy. The quest for sustainability in the built environment has now become a priority. The drive for carbon neutrality is at the forefront of the agenda, but there's an equally important factor for the legacy we leave behind. One of the most vital things we can do for the environment is create longevity, thus removing the need to demolish buildings that wouldn't need to be demolished if they'd been designed to be beautiful and long lasting.

A revolution is required, but this revolution doesn't need to involve mass social upheaval, destruction and vast expense (which, incidentally, were all features of building in the 20th century). We might call it the Realignment Revolution. It doesn't need government intervention or changes to the law. It requires nothing bureaucratic, cumbersome or costly. There's no obligation to march through the capital or organise demonstrations. All that's required is a shift of emphasis – a change of heart, if you will – to shed some indifference and capture some inspiration. To be mindful that the creation of a built environment that adequately encompasses the human condition and shows respect for generations to come is a sacred and necessary task. And to recognise that this sacred task can only be truly fulfilled when a person who's spent many years of their life dedicating themselves to the skill, knowledge and creativity it involves is allowed to do their work in the way it needs to be done.

And most of all, to entertain the possibility that three principles can help to change the world.

Good architecture is like a good therapy session, a good marriage, a good poem – gently and almost invisibly allowing you to be you, as flawed and as beautiful as you are.
ROBERT SULLIVAN, AUTHOR[4]

theme nine

The journey of a thousand miles starts with a single step.

notes

Introduction

1   David Goodhart, *Head, Hand, Heart,* Penguin Random House, Dublin, 2020.

2   Alessandra Latour, *Louis I Kahn: Writings, Lectures, Interviews,* Rizzoli International Publications, New York, 1991, p 59.

3   Christian Narkiewicz-Laine, 'Architecture of silence: Interview with Luis Barragán', *Global Design News,* 11 January 2021, https://www.globaldesignnews.com/architecture-of-silence-interview-with-luis-barragan (accessed 5 February 2024).

Chapter 1

1   Film: *The Matrix,* Warner Bros, 1999.

2   Rita Carter, *Mapping the Mind,* Phoenix, London, 2010, p 124.

3   Christopher Alexander, *The Nature of Order. Part One: The Phenomenon of Life. An Essay on the Art of Building and the Nature of the Universe,* The Center for Environmental Structure, Berkeley, 2002, pp 318–324.

Chapter 2

1   Ayn Rand, *The Fountainhead,* Penguin Random House, London, 2007 (first published 1943).

2   Film: *The Fountainhead,* Warner Bros, 1949.

3   Architects Registration Board, 'ARB publishes its latest Annual Report', 16 July 2020, https://www.arb.org.uk/arb-publishes-its-latest-annual-report-nr20 (accessed 5 February 2024).

4   Tarek Merlin, 'The vast majority of architects can't bid for public work: Something has to change', *Architects' Journal,* 20 February 2019, https://www.architectsjournal.co.uk/news/opinion/the-vast-majority-of-architects-cant-bid-for-public-work-something-has-to-change (accessed 5 February 2024).

5   Architects Registration Board, 'ARB publishes 2022 Annual Report and Financial Statements', 13 July 2023, https://arb.org.uk/arb-publishes-2022-annual-report-and-financial-statements (accessed 13 February 2024).

Chapter 3

1   Dame Judith Hackitt, *Building a Safer Future. Independent Review of Building Regulations and Fire Safety: Interim Report,* December 2017, p 5, https://assets.publishing.service.gov.uk media/5a82c507ed915d74e62378b9/Independent_Review_of_Building_Regulations_and_Fire_Safety_web_accessible.pdf (accessed 5 February 2024).

2   Dame Judith Hackitt, *Building a Safer Future. Independent Review of Building Regulations and Fire Safety: Final Report,* May 2018, https://assets.publishing.service.gov. uk/media/5afc50c840f0b622 e4844ab4/Building_a_Safer_ Future_-_web.pdf (accessed 5 February 2024).

3   Ibid., p 108.

Chapter 4

1   Georg Wilhelm Friedrich Hegel, *The Philosophy of History*, Dover Philosophical Classics, Mineola, NY, 2004 (first published 1837).

2   For example: E. J. C. van Leeuwen, K. A. Cronin and D. B. M. Haun, 'A group-specific arbitrary tradition in chimpanzees (Pan troglodytes)', *Animal Cognition*, Vol. 17, 2014, pp 1421–5, https:// www.doi.org/10.1007/s10071-014-0766-8 (accessed 5 February 2024).

3   Nicol Dynes, 'RIBA: Demolitions should be stopped to lower emissions', *realasset INSIGHT*, 12 July 2021, https://www.realassetinsight. com/2021/07/12/riba-demolitions-should-be-stopped-to-lower-emissions (accessed 5 February 2024).

4   Julie V. Iovine, Maria Robledo, Kim Johnson Gross and Jeff Stone, *Home (Chic Simple)*, Knopf, New York, 1993, p 43.

Chapter 5

1   Friedrich Engels, *The Condition of the Working Class in England,* Oxford University Press, Oxford, 2009 (first published in 1845).

2   Dominic Sandbrook, *White Heat: A History of Britain in the Swinging Sixties,* Abacus, London, 2007, p 4.

3   Brian Lund, *Understanding Housing Policy,* Policy Press, Bristol, 2017, p 37.

4   Ibid.

5   June Barnes, *What is the Future of High-Rise Housing? Examining the Long-Term Social and Financial Impacts of Residential Towers,* Levitt Bernstein, London, 2023, p 12.

6   Renzo Piano, Pritzker Architecture Prize acceptance speech, The White House, Washington, DC, 1998, https://www.pritzkerprize. com/sites/default/files/inline-files/1998_Acceptance%20Speech. pdf (accessed 6 February 2024).

Chapter 6

1   Film: *Jerry Maguire*, TriStar Pictures, Gracie Films, 1996.

2   Robert Bly, *A Little Book on the Human Shadow*, HarperCollins, New York, 1998, p 15.

3   Lee Grimsditch, 'People "clapped and cheered" as explosion ripped through precinct shoppers "couldn't wait to see the death of"', *Manchester Evening News*, 11 June 2023.

4   BBC News Online, 'Wind death in Leeds prompts tower safety fears', 11 March 2011, https://www. bbc.co.uk/news/uk-england-leeds-12717762# (accessed 6 February 2024).

5   Andrew Stuart, 'Why does the Beetham Tower hum in the wind?' *Manchester Evening News*, 10 February 2020.

6   Luis Barragán, Pritzker Architecture Prize acceptance speech, Dumbarton

Oaks, Washington, D.C., 1980,
https://www.pritzkerprize.com/
sites/default/files/inline-files/1980_
Acceptance%20Speech.pdf
(accessed 6 February 2024).

Chapter 7

1   Ministry of Housing, Communities
    and Local Government, *National
    Design Guide*, 2019 (updated 2021),
    https://www.gov.uk/government/
    publications/national-design-guide
    (accessed 6 February 2024).

2   Merlin Fulcher, 'Profession reacts to
    Prince Charles' 10 design principles',
    Architects' Journal, 22 December
    2014, https://www.architectsjournal.
    co.uk/news/profession-reacts-to-
    prince-charles-10-design-principles
    (accessed 13 February 2024).

Chapter 9

1   Christopher Booker, *The Seven
    Basic Plots: Why We Tell Stories*,
    Bloomsbury Continuum, London,
    2004.

2   Joseph Campbell, *The Hero with a
    Thousand Faces*, Fontana Press,
    London, 1993.

3   Alexander Purves, 'The persistence of
    formal patterns', *Perspecta*, Vol. 19,
    1982, pp 138–63.

4   Ibid.

Chapter 10

1   'Library Walk Link Building,
    Manchester: A three-dimensional
    abstract playfulness', *RIBA Journal*,
    20 April 2016, https://www.ribaj.
    com/buildings/library-walk-link-
    building-manchester (accessed
    6 February 2024).

Chapter 11

1   Richard Waite, '"Loveless execution":
    MVRDV breaks silence over Marble
    Arch Mound debacle',
    Architects' Journal, 8 February 2022,
    https://www.architectsjournal.co.uk/
    news/loveless-execution-mvrdv-
    breaks-silence-over-marble-arch-
    mound-debacle (accessed
    6 February 2024).

2   Alessandra Latour, *Louis I Kahn:
    Writings, Lectures, Interviews*, Rizzoli
    International Publications, New York,
    1991, p 117.

Chapter 12

1   Roger Ulrich, 'View through a window
    may influence recovery from surgery',
    Science, Vol. 224, Issue 4647,
    27 April 1984.

2   Rory Sutherland, *Alchemy: The Magic
    of Original Thinking in a World of
    Mind-Numbing Conformity*, WH Allen,
    London, 2020, p 60.

3   Christopher Alexander, *The Nature of
    Order. Part One: The Phenomenon
    of Life. An Essay on the Art of Building
    and the Nature of the Universe*,
    The Center for Environmental
    Structure, Berkeley, 2002, p 373.

4   Robert Sullivan, 'The architectural
    outsider', *Dwell*, 27 May 2009,
    https://www.dwell.com/article/the-
    architectural-outsider-c8ac1f58
    (accessed 6 February 2024).

index

image credits